We Still Have Him to Love

Overcome challenges in caregiving, achieve goals, travel and enjoy life

BILL DUWE

DEDICATION

For my wife, Lawana, who travels this journey with me.

Contents

ACKNOWLEDGEMENTS

I want to express my appreciation to those who helped make this book possible:

Susan, an occupational therapist from Ohio, for encouraging me to write a book. She met me on a cruise ship and convinced me our experiences would help parents who unexpectedly find they will be long term caregivers for their child.

Rick Butler for writing the foreword, reading an early draft and offering helpful suggestions.

Dave Finley, Elaine Maynard and Kim Pyles for reading draft copies and providing valuable input.

Janice Hays for being my editor.

Travis Duwe for designing the book cover.

Raychel Duwe for preliminary editing.

The Daily Citizen, Searcy, Arkansas, and Tulsa World for granting permission to reprint newspaper articles

My Wife, Lawana, for continually reading my writing and offering suggestions.

FOREWORD

Everything can change in the blink of an eye.

The accident Ray Duwe suffered in December 2000 altered not just his life but the lives of all those who love him.

I first met Ray through mutual college friends more than 30 years ago. The Ray I knew in college was honest, dependable, trustworthy and one of the funniest guys I've ever met.

In 2006, a group of Ray's former social club brothers arranged a surprise 40th birthday party for him. We told the stories that we'd told a thousand times and Ray laughed along with us. It was important for us to include his three children in that celebration. We felt they deserved to hear how we remembered their dad and they deserved to know there were former classmates now spread across the country who had been positively impacted by their father's friendship.

This book isn't just about Ray and the accident and its aftermath, though.

First, it serves as a guide of how to care for an incapacitated loved one. Second, it's a reminder that one's goals and plans might change but can still be reached.

Finally, it's a story of parents who love their son. Bill and Lawana Duwe have inspired and encouraged countless people with the examples they've shown for the past 16 years. Their love and devotion to Ray is evident in every word of this book.

By Rick Butler
October 27, 2017
Searcy, Arkansas

INTRODUCTION

Your life changes in an instant when a loved one is severely injured or disabled. You never expect this. You do not understand why. Will you be able to cope? What about the goals you had?

Our son, Ray, sustained a brain injury in an automobile accident. In this book, I want to use my experiences in 16 years of caregiving to help others in similar situations. I explain medical conditions in simple terms. I describe our challenges and rewards and explain how we keep our life on track. The value of support by friends and fellow Christians is emphasized along with a few inspiring examples from the Bible.

After the accident, my wife is alone when the neurologist comes to give us the latest report. He tells her Ray will be profoundly disabled. As he turns to leave, the doctor says, "At least you still have him to love." His words are the inspiration for the title of this book.

We pray what we share will be of value and a blessing in your life.

1 THE ACCIDENT

Proverbs 27:1 Do not boast about tomorrow, for you do not know what a day may bring.

My son, Ray, prepares for work on the morning of December 8, 2000. He helps his three children, Travis (8), Nicole (6) and Raychel (4), get ready for their day. The two older ones will go to school and the younger one to Grandma's house. Ray's wife, Shannon, is working.

When grandma (Ray's mother and my wife, Lawana) arrives to pick up Raychel, Ray opens the door. Winnie, their rat terrier, dashes out the door as she has done many times. The race is on to get her back in the house. The adults and the kids spend several minutes chasing the dog. Winnie seems to think it is great fun. Finally, they capture the escapee and prepare to resume their day.

As Lawana drives away, Ray is standing in the doorway holding Winnie in his arms. This is the last time she sees Ray standing.

Later that day, as I am driving home after work, a long line of cars blocks the road. We have plans to attend a Christmas party with our Sunday school class so I take an alternate route home. When I get home, my wife tells me Ray is late picking up his children. I tell her Ray is stuck either in the traffic jam or in an accident.

I decide to drive toward the traffic jam to try to find him. Before I can get out of the driveway, Lawana calls me back. The hospital has called to tell us Ray is in the emergency room. They have our telephone number on file for Ray. They give us the name of his case manager and tell us to come and ask for her by name. We call his wife at work and she drives straight to the ER. We load up the children and also head to the ER.

The case manager takes us to a private consultation room and explains Ray has been in an automobile accident. His neurologist tells us Ray has a brainstem contusion and a punctured lung. He is in a deep coma. He has no eye, verbal, or motor response. He is intubated and on a respirator. If he survives, the brainstem contusion will result in serious consequences. The punctured and deflated left lung is not a big concern. He has a few minor cuts, probably from flying glass, but no broken bones or other injuries.

Ray had fastened his seat belt and the airbag did deploy. The force of the crash caused his seat back to collapse so the restraints did not hold him. His head slammed back and forth causing a "closed head" injury. By "closed head," I mean the skull did not fracture. His injury was caused by a motion similar to "shaken baby syndrome" only more violent.

We call the Christmas party hosts to tell them. Word spreads quickly. During that long and stressful evening, at least 55 people come by the ER waiting room to support us.

Two police officers call me aside to explain the accident. Ray stopped behind a car that was waiting to turn left. A car hit Ray from behind, kicking him into the oncoming traffic. He was T-boned on the passenger side. The teenage driver of the car that originally hit him looked away for a moment to speak to his passenger. When he saw Ray, he braked and swerved, but he could not miss him. No alcohol was involved, and no one in either of the other two cars was injured. The boy did what we all do sometimes – he took his eyes off the road for only a few seconds.

Ray and his family 3 weeks before the accident

2 INTENSIVE CARE UNIT

Psalms 57:1 Have mercy on me, my God, have mercy on me, for in you I take refuge. I will take refuge in the shadow of your wings until the disaster has passed.

Ray moves to an intensive care unit with restricted visitor access. He looks terrible because the air from his punctured lung traps inside his skin. He looks puffy like the "Michelin Man" from the TV commercial. His skin feels like Rice Krispies when pressed. Only one person can visit him for a few minutes each hour. He has an ICP (intracranial pressure) monitor sticking out of his forehead. We are constantly checking it to see if it is rising as well as watching his numerous other monitors.

We find a little humor helps us cope. With the ICP monitor, tubing for respiration, and other tubes and wires, we joke that Ray looks like a Borg from Star Trek: The Next Generation. Borg are humans with various instruments and tubes attached to them. This light banter provides a relaxing moment in the midst of a serious situation. Sometimes there is simply a need for the emotional release of laughing or crying.

When a patient anywhere in the hospital needs resuscitation, a "Code Blue" announcement on the loud speaker gives the location of the patient. A "Code Blue" team responds immediately. It seems like a "Code Blue" call happens every day in Ray's ICU unit. It is a frightening experience each time because we can only wait to learn whether or not it is Ray.

Shannon, Lawana, and I live in the waiting room. At least one of us is always there. Ray continues to be in a coma. Our lives center on short visits to Ray's room. The outside world is not important. Oklahoma University's football team wins the National Championship. Election results are still in doubt between George W. Bush and Al Gore. Hanging chads are a big deal. Some days it snows so much we cannot leave the hospital.

Someone brings us a journal and suggests that we record daily events so we can remember treatments and progress. We record visitors and gifts they bring. We discuss who came the night of the accident and record their names.

Several other patients have family members living in the ICU waiting room at the same time. A sense of comradery develops among the various families. We spend Christmas in the waiting room, so we all decide to have a potluck meal in the waiting room. They ask me to lead a prayer. Lawana helps me by asking each family for the names of all the patients represented. I include each patient in the prayer. With this meal together, we are able to share the holiday with others. It is a heartwarming experience.

Ray and his family attend the Crosstown Church of Christ in Tulsa, Oklahoma; and Lawana and I attend the Broken Arrow Church of Christ in Broken Arrow, Oklahoma. We receive multiple visits daily from church friends, ministers, Ray's co-workers, high school and college friends from out-of-town. The two congregations bring food in for nine months, offer prayers, and do anything we need. A young family stays in Ray's house to take care of his children. The support helps to keep our spirits up. In our moments of deepest despair, God sends someone to provide the encouragement we need.

Ray slowly becomes responsive to light in his pupils. On January 8 (my birthday and one month after the accident), Ray opens his eyes for the first time. The length of his coma is an indicator of how limited his recovery will be. At this point we are optimistic about his recovery since all the movies and TV shows have the comatose person waking up and saying, "Where am I?" We joke that, since he is such a big sports fan, Ray will probably say instead, "What's the score?"

After six weeks, Ray is able to breathe on his own. The doctors cannot predict how much he will recover. They tell us that he has advantages for recovery. He is young (34 years old), athletic (He manages and plays on the church softball team.), and intelligent (He has an accounting degree from Harding University and an MBA from the University of Tulsa). We optimistically expect much more recovery than we get. We learn that most of his recovery will occur during the first six months. After six months, any recovery will happen very slowly. We search for studies to guide us in helping Ray recover. His neurologist tells us there are no studies and there never will be any because there will never be 100 people like Ray to study at one time.

Ray spends ten days in the rehab unit for therapy and family training. They loan a wheelchair to him. We learn how to care for him and how to do some physical therapy, skills which we absorb like a sponge.

Seven weeks after the accident, Shannon takes Ray home to care for him. Shannon's mother and sister move in to help as long as they can. Lawana and I also help several days every week. We recruit and train friends and church members to do physical therapy twice a day.

Ray and Shannon's marriage does not survive this catastrophe. This is frequently the outcome in Traumatic Brain Injury (TBI) situations. In November 2001, Shannon and I agree it is time to move Ray into our home. Lawana and I become his primary caregivers. All of the volunteers continue to help us. Ray's children stay with us every weekend and go to church with us. Sixteen years later, we still use volunteers, and Ray's children see him regularly.

Lesson Learned: I believe we need all of the support we receive. It is a great blessing to us. We are able to take advantage of the support by making our needs known to our friends and church family. Making our needs known is essential.

Tip: If possible, when people offer to help, let them. This can be a double blessing. The help given, however small, blesses you; and being useful blesses the helper.

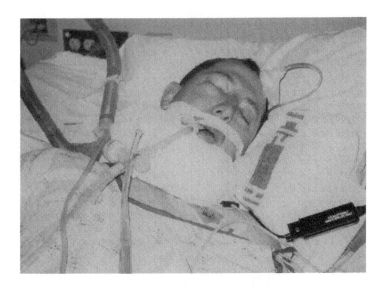

In ICU soon after the accident

3 LOCKED-IN SYNDROME

While Ray is in ICU, I research brainstem injuries in the hospital library and request reprints of a few articles. I learn that severe brainstem injury can disrupt eye movement, facial expression, speech, limb movement and other functions. If the upper brain is functioning, consciousness and cognitive functions operate normally.

In locked-in syndrome, nearly all voluntary muscles, except the eyes, are paralyzed. Usually eye blinking and vertical eye movements (up for yes, down for no) can be used for communication. In total locked-in syndrome even the eyes are paralyzed.

Observing Ray, I would say it is more complicated than just these two definitions. Ray is progressing in small increments and will probably continue to progress. For the first six months, Ray is totally locked-in, and eye contact is rare. Lawana describes it by saying, "The light is on, but no one is home." He is probably fully cognitive, but we cannot tell for sure. Even after six months, he can only make eye contact on his left side. He cannot move his eyes to the right. Even today, he cannot use vertical eye movement for

9

communication. It takes 13 years for him to be able to close his eyes for communication. He cannot always communicate by closing his eyes so it is not reliable enough to use for a serious medical diagnosis. He is somewhere between locked-in and totally locked-in.

Proverbs 17:22 A cheerful heart is good medicine....

August 2002: Ray is watching M.A.S.H. on TV, Lawana thinks she sees a smile on his face. She watches until she is convinced Ray is smiling. This is the first smile we see since the accident - a year and a half. It is significant in two ways. First, he is able to show emotion. Second, the emotion is an appropriate response to what he is seeing and hearing.

Family, friends, exercise volunteers, church friends and doctors all want to see Ray smile. Most people succeed in making him smile by telling jokes or funny stories. Sometimes we help so they can see his response. His children love to sing a silly song called "Magdalena Hagdalena" because it always gets a reaction.

This August the temperatures are dangerously hot in Oklahoma. The Oklahoma State University football team gives its players pickle juice to replenish their fluids in the heat. Two of Ray's exercise men begin to joke about the pickle juice. Ray thinks this is hilarious and smiles easily at the mere mention of pickle juice.

We find several things, like "pickle juice," that are sure to bring a smile to Ray's face. As you might expect, we overuse the jokes. Now we do not make extra effort to get him to smile. Smiles just happen naturally, but they are rare. We believe strong seizure medications are limiting the frequency of his smiles by suppressing all of his emotions.

Occasionally you can only recognize something funny on TV by reading text on the screen. We notice Ray responding correctly with a smile when this happens. We conclude Ray can read. Later we confirm his ability to read while working with the University of Tulsa Mary K. Chapman speech clinic.

Ray reacts to stories his friends tell about the past. Since most of those stories are humorous, Ray immediately begins to smile when he recognizes the story. This confirms Ray is aware of what is going on around him. Nevertheless, he is severely limited in his ability to interact with his surroundings. From his reaction to the past, we think his long-term memory is intact. We are not sure about his short-term memory, but we think it is functioning as well. We always encourage those around us to speak to Ray. It is difficult to talk with someone who cannot talk back to you, but worth the effort for the disabled person involved. It is important to remember that he is still a person and not a piece of furniture.

Tip: Hospital libraries will do literature searches for you on medical questions. Doctors can also request literature searches even when your loved one is not in the hospital.

4 SPASTICITY – SPLINTS, EARLY THERAPY

Ray has high spasticity in his initial ICU stay after the accident. Spasticity causes certain muscles to be tight (high tone) and causes involuntary movements. The injury to Ray's brainstem keeps him from controlling his muscles.

While in ICU, they use splints to try to keep Ray's hands from drawing up tight. They put special boots on his feet to try to keep them from pronating (turning inward). None of this is successful. Ray defeats the boots and the splints.

His left hand pulls up with his hand closed tightly. His right hand pulls down and closes tightly. His feet are stiff and turned in (pronated). He has involuntary movements of his arms head and legs. His legs draw up tightly and together. We remove the legs of his wheelchair because his knees will not straighten enough to use them. His feet pull up under the wheelchair. I am able to attach a padded plywood platform to the wheelchair where he could rest his legs. We use a small step stool for his feet.

Oral baclofen and other medications do not control his spasticity. Occupational therapists use serial casting to straighten his right elbow because it closes tightly. In serial casting, they open his elbow as much as they can and hold it while they put a rigid cast on it. After a few days, they remove the cast so they can open the elbow a little further and apply a new cast. This is somewhat effective. The elbow still will not open all the way. If they had not been able to open the elbow, it would be very hard to care for the skin inside the closed elbow.

Physical therapy is a continuing need. We are dealing with spasticity and trying to get as complete a recovery as possible. Physical therapy starts at home immediately after his release from the hospital. Ray only has his home hospital bed and a wheelchair. The therapist says he cannot do what he needs to do in the bed or the chair.

This presents a great opportunity for me to do something to help Ray. I need to build or buy a physical therapy table. I decide building a PT table was the quickest and most economical way to go. I find an upholstery supply company for the foam and vinyl to cover it. Then I build a plywood base to match. Before I upholstered it, four or five of us stood on the table to make sure it was strong enough. It is great therapy for me to be able to do something important. Fifteen years later, we still use this table twice a day to stretch Ray.

Speech therapy starts when he comes home from the hospital. They work on swallowing and vocal sounds. Due to lack of progress, we are not able to get insurance authorization for this to continue.

We hope and expect Ray will eventually speak and be able to eat normally. However, three months after the accident, we make an appointment with his ICU neurologist. The neurologist asks if Ray can talk. When we tell him not yet, he says if he is not talking by now, he doubts that he will ever talk. We continue to work toward the same goals, but with expectations that are more realistic.

Lesson Learned: Building the PT table is an opportunity to use my abilities to help Ray.

Tip: If you are not a handyman, you can look for a friend or someone in your church who will build something for you, like I built the PT table. This might provide someone an opportunity to help who cannot help in other ways. Many people want to help but do not know what to do.

5 WHEELCHAIR VAN

When it is time to release Ray from the hospital, they teach us to transfer Ray from his wheelchair to a car using a transfer board. This is not easy. Ray is 6 feet tall and weighs about 180 lbs. The wheelchair has removable arms, flat seat, and back cushions so he will slide to the side. It takes at least two people (a third person is helpful) to transfer Ray in or out of a car. The wheelchair does not collapse for transport and weighs about 100 lbs., so we have to lift it into the bed of our pickup truck.

We successfully take him home using this process. Since this is so difficult, we only transport Ray to doctor appointments and to the emergency room when needed. Since Ray cannot sit in a regular folding wheelchair, we always take his wheelchair in our pickup truck.

Transportation is a critical need, so I begin to look for a better solution. I have no knowledge in this area. We have a minivan, so my first thought is to use a ramp to roll Ray into the minivan. Of course, I would have to remove the middle seats. Ramps are cheap so this would be economical. Then I decide to check the headroom in the van. Big problem, Ray is 5 or 6 inches too tall to fit in the van when seated in his wheelchair.

When I was a young engineer, I was showing an older engineer a sketch of one of my ideas. He suspected it would not work so he told me: "You can make anything work in a sketch." Sure enough, when I measured everything it would not work. I think that goes double when dealing with wheelchairs. You have to measure everything.

I still think the ramp idea is a good economical solution. Armed with the measurement of Ray's height while he is sitting in his wheelchair, I go to a used car lot to measure the headroom in some full size vans. Ray is an inch or two too tall for even a full size van. That means we will need a high top van. Another reality is that the floor height in a full size van will require a long ramp to get him in it.

By now, I learn a little about wheelchair lifts for vans. The transportation solutions are beginning to look more expensive. Even though Ray has medical insurance, it is not going to buy a van for us. I begin to look for used wheelchair lifts in the want ads. I find a few but when I look at them, I am not confident that I can install one in a van, even if I own a suitable van.

About this time, we have to take Ray to the emergency room. We successfully get him into the ER. The hospital does not admit him, so we begin to transfer him back into the car. He suddenly arches his back and begins to fall. Fortunately, a security guard comes to our rescue and saves him from falling to the ground.

Now we are desperate for a wheelchair van. The next day I see a wheelchair van advertised in the newspaper. It is $6,900. I call. The owner's mother passed away the previous week. It is a high top van with a basic "drawbridge" type of lift. It is an older van with 87,000 miles on it. The owner needs the $6,900 to pay off the loan on it. We look at it and buy it on the spot.

We drive this van for two years. The biggest problem we have is an engine fire with Ray in the van. It is scary. The fire department takes Ray home for us. It takes several weeks to get the van repaired. We make a few road trips in it, with and without Ray's kids. We improve it by having the side doors raised to make it easier to get Ray in and out.

After two years, we can afford a new van, and we certainly have a long-term need that justifies it. It takes about three months to get the full-size van we want built for us. When we get the new van, we advertise the old one in the newspaper for $6,900. A woman looks at it and buys it on the spot for $6,900 to transport her husband.

On our road trips, Ray watches recorded movies. Some movies he has seen many, many times, but they are his favorites: *The Natural, Hoosiers, Field of Dreams, The Rookie* and *The Blind Side.* Do you see a trend here? He is definitely a sports fan. At home, we usually tune the TV to sports. Ray is a fan of the St. Louis Cardinals, OU football, TU football and basketball, and Thunder basketball, but he watches whoever is on.

We drive this van for 14 years. We replace the fuel pump twice, the transmission once, and the air conditioner compressor twice. I accidentally run over a piece of curb, bending the wheelchair lift under the van beyond repair. The replacement cost is $10,000 and we are without the van for two months. Fortunately, I have coverage for the lift added onto my auto insurance for the van. It is very expensive to replace a van, so we keep it well maintained. After 14 years and 100,000 miles, we decide to replace it with a new one. Because it is in excellent condition, we are able to sell it for $14,000.

We decide to get another full-size van instead of a minivan. Ray's large wheelchair fits better in a full-size van. In addition, a full-size van has enough luggage space for the equipment we need when traveling. Since most wheelchair vans today are modified minivans, we purchase a full-size van and have it converted to a wheelchair van.

Tip: You can purchase used expensive equipment at a considerable savings. People who no longer need equipment frequently place want ads in local newspapers. People also donate wheelchairs, walkers, etc. to churches, so you might get free equipment from them. A notice on social media might locate free or low cost equipment.

Ray's 2017 wheelchair van with wheelchair lift lowered to receive Ray in his wheelchair.

6 BACLOFEN PUMP

Six months after Ray's accident, his spasticity and high muscle tone are still a major problem. Since we have tried more than one oral medication, we are able to get an evaluation for a baclofen pump. They inject baclofen into his spinal column to see if his spasticity and muscle tone reduces. The results are positive, so we schedule Ray to get a pump implanted. The doctor surgically implants the pump in his abdomen. Baclofen pumps through a catheter that runs under the skin into the spinal column. The pump is refilled by injecting baclofen into the pump port. A battery inside the pump housing powers the pump. Battery life is about five years. When the battery is near the end-of-life, the pump is surgically replaced.

The baclofen pumping rate is set low when first implanted. A computer programs the pump via a small wand placed on the skin over the pump. We begin weekly visits to the doctor and gradually increase the flow rate. There is no standard flow rate because each patient is unique. After a few weeks, we gradually see positive results.

At one of the early visits, I ask the doctor if she wants to increase his flow rate. She tells me it is up to me. She says I need to take control of Ray's medical treatment because no doctor will know him as well as I know him. This is a wakeup call that helps me understand my role.

We continue to increase his baclofen flow rate to as high as we think Ray can tolerate. Even at this rate, he still has high muscle tone in his upper body. The muscle tone in his legs reduces to a good level. We are able, with continued stretching of his leg muscles, to get his knees nearly straight. This is amazing because the surgeon who implanted the pump could not straighten Ray's legs while fully sedated. Therefore, the surgeon doubts we will ever be able to straighten them.

When his pump is near end-of-life, his doctor thinks he should get a pump with the catheter placed higher in his spine. Some patients are seeing better results in their upper body muscle tone with the higher catheter placement. In 2005, his new pump is implanted. Ray does get better results with the new pump and catheter.

In 2007, Ray goes into the hospital with pneumonia. His lung function is weak and he has a hard time recovering. The pulmonary doctor thinks the high level of baclofen is reducing muscle tone in his lungs and compromising their function. We decide to reduce the pump rate 40% total by reducing it 20% immediately, then completing the reduction two days later. Ray adjusts to the lower level easily and recovers from the pneumonia. His muscle tone in his arms and legs is fine at the lower rate, so we keep this rate until 2009.

From July 2009 to February 2010, Ray enters the hospital four times with pneumonia and begins to have seizures. Thinking a lower rate of Baclofen will help his lung function, we begin reducing it gradually. By the end of 2009, we reduce it to 50% of what it was at the beginning of 2009. His muscle tone is fine, and he is free of pneumonia until November 2010.

He is back in the hospital with pneumonia in November 2010, December 2010, and February 2011. Since he has been able to adjust to significant reductions in Baclofen, we begin to think he might not need Baclofen any more. Knowing it is safer to reduce Baclofen slowly, we ask the doctor to reduce his Baclofen 10% a week to see how low we can get it. We hope to eliminate it. Since the reduction is 10% each week, the amount reduced becomes smaller each week. It takes eight months to reduce it low enough to turn it off. We remove the pump in December 2011.

The Baclofen gives us amazing results for several years. We will probably never know why he does not need it now. It could be a long-term benefit from the custom seating. Or, it could be long term healing from his original injury. We stretch his limbs twice a day on the PT table. This has noticeable benefits also. It probably is a combination of all three. I think the benefit of custom seating is significant because he tightens up when he is in an uncomfortable position.

Lesson Learned: By understanding and being active in treatment plans, I am able to be a better advocate for Ray. Since I see all the doctors, I am frequently in the best position to suggest modification or elimination of treatments.

7 OUR FIRST ROAD TRIP

My social club from Harding University has a reunion in 2003. We decide to attend. This will require us to drive five hours and stay in a college dorm room. The room is actually a two-bedroom suite with a living room so it is large enough for Ray and us.

At this point, we have a wheelchair van for transporting Ray in his wheelchair. We also have a Hoyer lift for transferring him between bed and wheelchair and an alternating pressure air mattress to prevent bedsores. The Hoyer lift will disassemble so we can take it in the van. We cannot take his home hospital bed. Since he has to have his upper body elevated when he sleeps, we need more than a regular twin bed.

We decide to search for a portable hospital bed. After many internet searches, I find an aluminum folding bed that weighs only 19 lbs. It is similar to an aluminum camp cot except each end raises. The head has three positions, very similar to his hospital bed. The leg section raises without bending the knees, which is different from his home bed, but we decide it is the best solution. We order it for $175. We have used it on many road trips. His alternating pressure mattress deflates and fits in a duffle bag for easy travel. At our destination, it inflates and straps easily to the aluminum bed.

Now all we have to do is pack everything we need in the van and make the trip. Packing turns out to be a major project all its own. We make a list of everything we need and include extra supplies in case we have a problem that delays our return.

Unloading and setting up in the dorm room is not trivial. We make several trips from the van to the room just to get it all unloaded. The bed then is set up with the air mattress. It takes 45 minutes for the mattress to inflate, so we arrive early enough to set up before the reunion activities.

Setting up the room requires careful thought to provide placement of the wheelchair and bed to allow space to transfer Ray with the Hoyer lift. This is always a challenge, especially in hotel rooms. Occasionally we lift him out of his chair in the hallway and then move him into the room with the lift to lower him onto his bed. A few times, we have asked the hotel to remove some furniture from our room to allow more space.

This packing list develops into two lengthy lists – one for short trips and one for long trips. We allow a week to gather and pack everything. We sometimes experience delays in our trips, so we always pack extra. Even with these lists, we occasionally forget some important items. For example, once we forgot the pump for the air mattress. The hotel where we are staying loans us a mattress from one of their roll-a-way beds to put on our aluminum bed. Without the air mattress, we turn Ray every two hours during the night to prevent bedsores. So far, we are always able to work around any forgotten item.

Is the trip worth it? The reunion is nice, but nobody from my college days comes. In fact, I win the award for being the oldest club member attending. It is not a success in terms of renewing college friendships. However, it is very important for us to successfully make our first trip and know it is very possible to travel.

Lesson Learned: Travel is possible, even with severe disabilities. Careful research and planning help us prepare for most travel difficulties. Each trip brings its own challenges, and you must learn to go with the flow and expect the unexpected.

Tip: If you wish you had something and you do not know if it exists, search the internet. I did not know if a portable bed existed for our need but I was able to find it after several searches.

8 CUSTOM SEATING

For a while, Lawana takes Ray to a community college class of physical therapy assistants once a week. They give Ray physical therapy under the supervision of their instructor. This is mutually beneficial. He is still in his original seating. Even with the Baclofen pump, his muscle tone is still high. The instructors encourage us to contact Oklahoma University to evaluate him for custom seating. Custom seating will support him better than his flat cushions and result in a reduction of muscle tone. It will also provide better protection against pressure sores.

OU agrees that Ray qualifies for custom seating. Over a period of 2-3 years, they make three combinations of seat bottom and back cushions. Finally, we have a very successful set, which we use for about ten years. We still use those cushions as our back-up set.

OU also overhauls his wheelchair to be better for Ray and for us. They widen it two inches for the custom cushions. The cushions are wide with a deep contour so Ray fits down into them for much better support and stability. Wheels 12" in diameter and 2" wide with a rear brake replace the narrow width large diameter wheels. We actuate the brake from the rear with our feet. This is much safer for Ray and easier for us. The original brakes are individual front hand levers. Since Ray cannot propel the chair or apply the brakes, the original tall wheels and front hand brakes are inferior to the upgrade. OU also adds a high quality headrest.

Not only do we have a vastly improved wheelchair, we now have a relationship with the OU physical and occupational therapy school in Tulsa and Oklahoma City that continues to this day. OU invites us every year to share our story with the PT and OT students in their annual stroke/brain injury seminar.

We try another type of custom cushions but Ray develops a red spot in less than 20 minutes. OU stops making custom cushions, so I search for another source for that type of custom cushion in Oklahoma. Unable to find a new source, I am able to learn how to make plaster molds and duplicate the OU cushions. OU and the foam manufacturer are a great help in my learning process. It takes me three tries to get a good bottom cushion. With this learning curve, I am able to get a good back cushion in one try. He can sit in these cushions for 12 hours without a red spot. This is especially important when we travel.

Lesson Learned: A church member recommended we talk to a physical therapist he knew. The physical therapist then recommended we contact an instructor at the community college. We learned we could find valuable resources when we follow-up on suggestions for help.

Tip: Local colleges and universities may have resources available free or for a reduced rate.

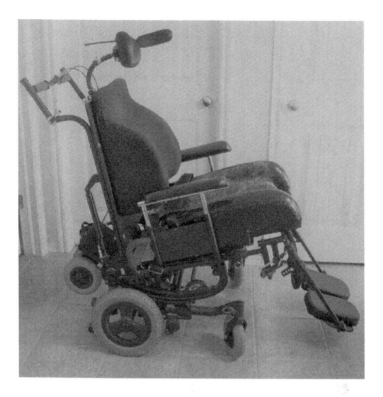

I added an assist motor to the wheelchair. It is easy to remove and replace, so I only use it when I know I will be pushing it up steep slopes or on grass. I put two door hinges under the center of the seat cushion so I can tilt it left and right to shift his weight. This makes the seat more comfortable and helps prevent pressure sores. The cushions are custom molded to fit and support him.

We had a problem with Ray's head and body severely leaning to the left. A friend made a bracket for me to mount an adjustable headrest on the left side to hold his head and begin to work it back straight. A home health physical therapist worked with him for two months to get it nearly vertical. OU also made an improved custom seat back that held his body more vertical. We have been able to keep him fairly vertical with the custom seating and the side headrest.

9 OUR FIRST CRUISE

In 2005, Lawana reads in a magazine that cruising is a good vacation for people in wheelchairs and suggests we take a cruise to Alaska. This is a bold idea. We have successfully taken a few road trips but we have not considered flying with Ray. The cruise would depart from Seattle. Driving from Broken Arrow to Seattle would take us five hard days of driving so we decide to investigate flying.

I call Ray's ex-wife for advice. She is a gate agent for Continental Airlines. She assures me air travel is possible. She explains we take Ray to the door of the airplane in his wheelchair. Then airline personnel lift him out of his wheelchair into an "aisle wheelchair". An "aisle wheelchair" is very narrow with three straps to fasten an individual to it. Then they roll him backwards down the aisle to his seat. They lift him into his seat. His wheelchair is gate checked and stored with the luggage. When we land, they bring his wheelchair to the door of the airplane. Then they lift him into another "aisle wheelchair" to bring him out of the plane. Then they lift him back into his wheelchair. On this flight, we will change planes in Denver, so we will roll him to the next gate and repeat the process.

An "aisle wheelchair" is very uncomfortable because it so small. Since Ray is a full quadriplegic, his wheelchair has custom cushions in it to support him. It also tilts back so he sits in a comfortable reclining position. In the plane, Ray sits in a regular airline seat. It does not support him well nor does it recline enough to make Ray very comfortable. His drooling problem is even worse while sitting upright. Since he is not sitting in his custom cushions pressure sores are a concern. In later years, I make a custom cushion to place into the airline seat to minimize the pressure sore concern. In short, airline travel is possible but we avoid it if we can.

We arrange the assistance needed from the airline in advance. The airlines are always very helpful to us. We also learn the airlines do not charge luggage fees for Ray's wheelchair or any of his assistive equipment. We have as many as seven extra pieces in addition to normal suitcases. The extras include cases of food, his mattress, his portable lift, his Smart vest that takes two cases, and the wedge for elevating his head. We remove the arms, legs and headrests from the wheelchair to prevent damage in the baggage compartment. We carry them in a duffle bag

We book our hotel through the cruise line. We purchase transfers to the airport, then to the ship, and then back to the airport when we return to Seattle. We specify we need wheelchair accessible transportation. The cruise line offers wheelchair accessible transfers at no extra charge.

A big problem is transferring Ray from his chair to a bed and back to his chair. We need to do this in the hotel, and at least twice a day on the ship. On the ship, we think ship personnel can help us lift and transfer him. We quickly find that the cruise line will not allow their personnel to lift Ray. Probably this is a liability issue.

Our second thought is to find a couple to book the same cruise and help with the lifting. We strike out on this plan also.

Then we discover durable medical equipment companies rent equipment to use on cruises. This plan works. The company delivers a patient lift to our hotel room in Seattle. We use it the night before the cruise, and then send it with our luggage to our cabin on the ship. We use it throughout the cruise. The durable equipment company tells us to leave it in our cabin so they can pick it up on the dock. For later cruises, we purchase a lightweight folding lift that gives us good service.

We can take his alternating pressure air mattress on the ship, but not our aluminum portable bed. Therefore, we buy an inflatable wedge to use under his head. We place the air mattress on top of the ship's mattress with the inflatable wedge in between. This works but it is wobbly. On later cruises, we discover we can ask our cabin steward to store the ship's mattress. Then we strap his mattress to the bed frame for a more stable bed.

My search for a better wedge is futile. After our second cruise, I decide to build an adjustable wedge out of wood to raise Ray's head. We use this for several cruises, but since we have no way to raise his legs, he slips down in the bed during the night.

Recently I built a folding plywood assembly that is the full width and length of the mattress. With this, we raise his knees and his head to the same position we use at home. I used 3/8" plywood so it weighs 30 lbs.; and it folds to fit in a mirror-shipping box. It is a little awkward, but we carry it in our van and send it with our luggage to our cabin. This is a better solution because his sleeping position is almost exactly like his bed at home.

On the day of the cruise, we place our luggage in the designated area then wait patiently for our wheelchair transportation. This turns out to be a large bus with a wheelchair lift. The driver loads us first so we can be settled in before the rest of the passengers board. When we reach the port, he drops off the other passengers first and then takes us to the wheelchair entrance. We go to a special check-in desk for passengers requiring assistance. A crewmember assists us up the gangway to the ship.

The crewmember escorts us to our cabin. On the way, I begin to get concerned because the cabin doors are obviously too small for Ray's wheelchair. Pleasantly we find our cabin door is wide enough and the room is large enough for us move Ray about and transfer him.

Moving about the ship is easy once we learn to avoid the cabin hallways. The cabin stewards usually have cleaning carts in the cabin hallways. We would have to move each cart to have enough room for the wheelchair. The hallways in the public areas are much wider. The ship has forward, middle and aft elevators. Our room is near the forward elevators, so we usually take the forward elevator to deck seven. It has only public areas. Then we go to the middle or aft elevators if we need an elevator to another deck.

We have assigned seating in the main dining room on deck 6. It can only be reached by the aft elevators so we leave our cabin, take the forward elevator to deck 7, roll to the aft elevators, then go down to deck 6. They assign us to a large round table for nine passengers. It is by a window and very far from the dining room entrance. It takes a while for one of the waiters to weave Ray through the tables to our table.

We enjoy visiting with the other three couples at our table, but we now choose anytime dining in the other dining rooms. The menu in these dining rooms is the same as the main dining room. In these dining rooms, they find a small table for us near the entrance so it is easier to reach our table. They usually select a suitable table and keep it for us every night. Since we usually eat alone, we are able to finish early for an early show.

The Cruise Director's staff conducts Trivia and other team games for the passengers. We enjoy these games and meet several other passengers doing this.

This first cruise to Alaska is along the Inside Passage. The ports are near the small towns. The sidewalks and streets are fairly wheelchair accessible, so we are able to take Ray ashore and enjoy the ports.

Tours that are wheelchair accessible are few, but we book an accessible tour to Mendenhall glacier. Unfortunately, we experience one of the variables of cruising – bad weather with rough seas. It is too rough to dock, so the captain anchors off shore. Tenders transport passengers ashore. A tender is a small 100-passenger boat that is not wheelchair accessible. It looks like we will miss our tour. Fortunately, the waters calm after a few hours, and we are able to dock. Knowing we are disappointed, the ship tour personnel arrange a special tour for us to the Mendenhall Glacier. The weather is rainy, but we appreciate the extra effort by the tour staff. We learn two lessons: we have to be flexible for weather problems, and the tour desk will make extra effort to help us. These two lessons ease our frustrations on future cruises.

We are apprehensive before our first cruise because there are so many unknowns. Cruising has several advantages compared to a road trip. After we are on the ship, we stay in the same room instead of moving from hotel to hotel. Our handicap room on the ship is usually more accessible than a hotel room. We can usually access the dining rooms, entertainment, and other activities. On the road, we load Ray into his van to go to a restaurant, etc. When we reach our destination, parking, weather and seating are frequently difficult.

With all these advantages, cruising has become the preferred vacation for the three of us. We always use Princess Cruises. Since we have completed several cruises on Princess, we have earned perks such as free internet and free laundry. We have completed 19 cruises, including the Caribbean several times, Canada/New England twice, Hawaii twice, Alaska three times, California Coastal, and Mexico. Flying overseas would be too uncomfortable for Ray due to the long length of the flights, so we only cruise out of North American ports. To reach our ship, we have driven to Los Angeles twice and Fort Lauderdale several times. We have the time and prefer to drive rather than fly.

Handicap accessibility is better in the U.S. and Canada. We feel blessed to live where access is a requirement for the handicapped. It still is not perfect, but it is better than in some countries. One time on board ship, a young Filipino waiter asks about the equipment we use. She tells us her father had a stroke and cannot even get out of bed. We tell her to check the internet for products to help him but wonder if they would be available or affordable in the Philippines.

Lesson Learned: Much of what we learn about travel is difficult to grasp until we actually experience it. It is very much worth the leap of faith for us. After our first big trip, travel becomes easier to plan. Even after nineteen cruises, we experience unexpected difficulties but are better equipped to handle the challenges.

Tip: The airlines and cruise lines are helpful. Ask for the Access Department. Do not be afraid to ask questions and request help when needed. This should be done well in advance of your trip, but be sure you know whom to call when problems arise while in transit, too.

This is a piece of the Mendenhall glacier in Juneau, Alaska. We visited it in 2011 on an Alaskan cruise.

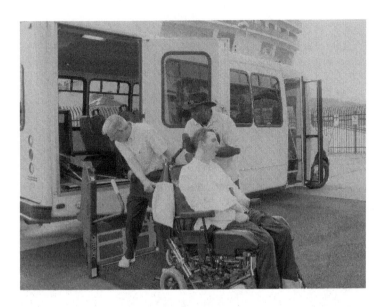

Loading Ray into a tour bus in St. Thomas, U.S. Virgin Islands on a Caribbean cruise in 2012.

Ray and Lawana viewing Waimea Canyon on the island Kauai in the Hawaiian islands in 2013. We were able to get to it on an accessible bus.

10 TROUBLE ON THE ROAD

Ecclesiastes 4:9-10 Two are better than one, because they have a good return for their labor: If either of them falls down, one can help the other up. But pity anyone who falls and has no one to help them up.

In October of 2005, we take Ray and his children up to Pleasant Hill, Missouri, to visit our daughter, Regina, and her family. The next day we all visit a pumpkin patch in a nearby town. The grandchildren enjoy the corn maze and various amusements; and they pick out pumpkins to take home. We have a good visit and head back on Sunday afternoon. The van begins to act up, and we limp into the parking lot of a hotel along the highway in Carthage, Missouri. We all go into the lobby and explain what happened. The hotel is not very full, so they offer us two adjoining rooms for the price of one for Sunday night. We unload the van and call for a tow truck. I call Shannon to tell her I cannot get the kids back to her for school on Monday. We unpack, set up Ray's bed, and settle in for the night.

While we are waiting for a diagnosis on the van Monday, we remember that Jim and Jane Murray live close by in Diamond, Missouri. A church friend had introduced us to the Murrays because their son had a serious brain injury from an accident several years before. The experiences they shared with us were very helpful. Jane is very active in MADD (Mothers against Drunk Driving) because a drunk driver hit their son. We had not seen them in quite a while.

They are only 15 miles away from us, so Jane volunteers to pick up the kids and have them spend the day. Jane, a former schoolteacher, decides the children need an educational experience since they are missing school. She takes them to the nearby George Washington Carver Monument. Later Jim and Travis go fishing in their pond. Travis catches an 11 pound 28 inch long catfish. This is definitely the largest fish Travis ever caught. They have a very enjoyable day instead of spending it in a hotel room.

The van needs a new fuel pump and will not be ready until Wednesday. We do not have enough food and supplies for Ray. The kids need to be in school. The Murrays loan me a car for the evening to take the children home and pick up supplies. I make a quick trip to Broken Arrow and back. Again, God's family is blessing us.

Stranded in our hotel, our only easy source of meals is an Arby's next door. Arby's is one of our favorite fast food restaurants, but Arby's three meals a day can be monotonous. Once the service department fixing our van has to give me a ride so I can show them documentation in the van. On the way back to the hotel, we stop at a KFC so I can get different meals. When the van is not available, we realize how important it is to us.

The van is ready Wednesday afternoon, so we are able to return home.

Lesson Learned: When you are in a difficult situation, church friends or acquaintances often can solve the problem or know someone who can.

11 ADVENTURES IN WYOMING

On our way back from Yellowstone National Park in 2006, we make a side trip to Independence Rock in Wyoming. This is a huge dome-shaped granite rock on the old Oregon Trail. It is 136 feet tall, 1,900 feet long and 700 feet wide. Wagon trains tried to reach the rock by July 4, Independence Day. If they did not, the early snows could block the mountain passes. It is amazing to see wagon ruts still visible in the ground.

Travis, Nicole, and I climb to the top. We see several names and dates carved into the surface by early travelers. It seems that most of the dates ranged from July 2 to July 10. I believe many dates were in the 1840's and 1850's. Raychel, the youngest, is not able to climb very far in her flip-flops, so she climbs back down crying because she cannot keep up with us. Lawana consoles her and loans her shoes to Raychel. She climbs up by herself and meets us near the top, very proud of her accomplishment. Lawana and Ray patiently wait down below and watch us as we climb.

This adventure is a wonderful memory. Sometimes you cannot predict which experience will be the most memorable.

The next day we stop for Sunday worship in Cheyenne, Wyoming. This church has a disabled military veteran member who uses a wheelchair, so they have a nice ramp. This ramp is impressive in size and construction. It is a wood structure built alongside the building. The first section of the ramp is about 30 feet long and leads to a landing where it makes a 180 degree turn; then it continues another 30 feet. At the top, the church has an entry door. When we enter the door, we are at the front of the auditorium. Members greet us warmly and encourage us to sit on the front row because it is the easiest place for us. After service, we meet the military veteran and probably everyone else, since it is a small congregation.

After much visiting, we prepare to be on our way. We are parked on the street next to a sidewalk. We load Ray in the van and try to stow the lift. Ray's weight in the van forces the lift down against the concrete, which prevents the lift from stowing. It has a safety switch that keeps it from stowing under load so it will not stow with a wheelchair on it. This is normally a good feature; but in this case, we cannot get the lift to move at all.

Some of the church members see we have a problem and come to help. After discussing possible solutions, I decide that, if we have enough help to push on the side of the van to tilt it perhaps we can raise the lift enough to free it. Someone calls church members, some of whom have already left, and they come back. Men and women lend a hand, and we all push against the side of the van. After a couple of tries, we are able to tilt it and free the lift.

Our new friends invite us to go to lunch. We have to drive clear across town, but we enjoy a good meal with

WE STILL HAVE HIM TO LOVE

some good fellowship. Another instance of finding help when needed from fellow Christians.

Lesson Learned: Attending church when traveling is usually uplifting. Frequently you will find a connection to someone from your hometown.

12 SCREAMING

Seven years after his accident, Ray wakes us in the middle of the night with four or five very loud screams. This is very startling, because he has not made any vocal sounds since the accident. A few days later, he screams again. He begins to scream four or five times in a row at random times, including during church. Always screaming at the top of his lungs.

Ray is able to use his scream effectively, if he feels threatened. He can be very intimidating. On one cruise he feels threatened going through security to re-board the ship. The inspectors separate him from us when they start to pat him down. When he screams and flails his arms and legs, they stop. When we get to him to calm him down, security just tells us to take him onto the ship without checking him further.

One of his doctors requests a literature search to check for other brain injury patients who began to scream or vocalize after several years. She finds one case where a woman begins screaming after 14 years. She then begins to speak words after another six years. It might be possible that Ray may speak in the future.

Ray's vocalization is now in its ninth year. He makes more controlled sounds now. The screams are almost never at the top of his lungs. In the past few months, he is able to say "ah" on command two or three times. We believe these are signs of real progress. Recovery in this area is very slow for Ray.

Lesson Learned: Discuss sudden changes with your doctor. They may be significant.

13 NUTRITION

After several tries, we finally find a medical food (formula) that Ray tolerates well, with little or no stomach residuals. However, in 2008, two companies merge and consolidate their product lines. The combined company discontinues Ray's food. His food supplier recommends a food for Ray. It looks OK to Ray's doctor and us, so they deliver a 30-day supply.

Immediately Ray starts having significant stomach residuals. Ray does not adjust to the new food, so after a few days I ask his supplier to find some of his old food to use while we sort this out. They find enough for about two weeks. He immediately adjusts back to the old food. This reinforces our belief that the problem is the new food. It is comforting to know we are working on the right thing.

Our supplier's dietitian selects another food. They send a 30-day supply of it. Ray does not adjust to it either. Now I am talking directly to the dietitian. She has no idea why Ray is not tolerating the new foods. They look nutritionally equivalent to her. This is looking desperate. There is no more of the old food available.

We need a quick solution, so I call the manufacturer and explain the sequence of events to their dietitian. She immediately identifies the problem. She explains the old food contained only protein from milk sources. The two new foods contain only protein from soy sources. She says they have run into this before. Ray probably does not tolerate soy protein. She tells me how to identify the protein sources in the list of ingredients on the food labels. She then recommends a food in their product line that only contains milk protein.

Our supplier has this food and delivers a 30-day supply. Bingo, it works. I now know how to identify foods that Ray probably will be able to tolerate. This proves to be very helpful.

We are doing fine with the food until 2015. I receive a shipment of food with labels that look a little different. The name of the food is unchanged, but the front label says it has soy protein. Sure enough, when I compare the old and new labels, I see the main protein source is now soy. I immediately call our supplier and explain Ray does not tolerate soy protein. They are unaware of the change in protein. They find a two-week supply of the old label food while I am on the phone. They courier it to me the next morning to use while we find a new food.

We select a new food from the same manufacturer that has only milk protein in it. Bingo again – it works. We are fine again until 2016. The sequence repeats again – new label, this time all protein changed to soy. Our supplier is caught unaware of the change again. They find some old food for us to use while we look for a new food. When the new food is located, I suggest they call the manufacturer to see if they have plans to change this one also. The manufacturer says they plan to keep this one formula with milk protein for patients like Ray who cannot tolerate soy protein. It must be uncommon to be intolerant of soy protein. This food works for Ray, so we should be OK for a while. Nevertheless, with food, we need to keep reading the ingredient labels carefully.

Lesson Learned: Hospitals have in-patient and outpatient dietitians available at no charge. Medical food suppliers also have dietitians. You can call your medical food manufacturer and talk to a dietitian.

14 THE PNEUMONIA YEARS

2 Corinthians 4:16-17 Therefore we do not lose heart. Though outwardly we are wasting away, yet inwardly we are being renewed day by day. For our light and momentary troubles are achieving for us an eternal glory that far outweighs them all.

From July 2009 to February 2011, Ray is in the hospital with pneumonia seven times. During this time, Ray has several medical issues. His primary injury is a brainstem contusion. The brainstem connects your brain to the spinal cord, which explains why he is a quadriplegic. The messages for his arms and legs just cannot get through his brainstem. The brainstem also controls body temperature and breathing which are two of Ray's issues.

Ray's respiration is not normal. During this time, the doctors discover his brain receptors that control his breathing sense only his blood oxygen level. Normally your brain receptors sense the blood carbon dioxide level. If your carbon dioxide level gets too high, you breathe more to get rid of the carbon dioxide. If Ray is breathing room air, his carbon dioxide level is usually high, but not high enough to be a major problem. However, if you give Ray pure oxygen he does not have to breathe very often to keep his blood oxygen level high enough. Very soon, his blood carbon dioxide level will be dangerously high because he is not breathing often enough to expel the carbon dioxide.

This has ramifications when Ray is in the hospital. Hospital personnel give extra oxygen in numerous situations that Ray may experience. It is important to stop them. Sometimes I have to be very persuasive to stop them. His hospital records now show oxygen as an allergy, so this helps me convince them. Normally respiratory therapists give all breathing treatments with pure oxygen. They have to give Ray's breathing treatments with room air, so they have to bring an air valve into his room. I like them to remove the oxygen valve, but they will not always remove it. Even if they do remove it, respiratory therapists always have oxygen valves with them. They can have oxygen hooked up so quickly you might not notice at first. I usually get a sign taped over the oxygen port to block it.

We know Ray's body temperature regulation is poor even before these hospitalizations. Ray has gone into hypothermia with body temperature as low as 88 degrees F. It takes several hours under a Bair Hugger to bring his body temperature up to normal. A Bair Hugger is a blanket warmed by forcing precisely controlled warm air through it.

We did recognize hypothermia to be a major problem, but we did not consider regularly running 2 or 3 degrees below normal a problem. The definition of hypothermia is a temperature of 95 degrees F or lower. Ray is living close to hypothermia most of the time. Since Ray is having pneumonia on a repeated basis, his primary care doctor theorizes that his low body temperature is lowering his resistance to infection. The doctor's idea is that since body temperature normally rises to fight infection, then a higher body temperature may help him resist infection. To accomplish this, we start dressing him in warmer clothes and adding blankets as necessary to keep his body temperature up.

Our first goal is to keep him at 98.6 degrees F. This is unachievable, so we settle for keeping him at 97.0 or above. In most public areas this usually requires a long sleeved shirt, a blanket around the back of his neck, and three blankets covering him from his neck to his feet. At home or in a hotel, ship cabin or hospital room, we adjust the room temperature higher so we do not need as many blankets.

We use Dulcolax to regulate his bowel movements. His body temperature is too low to dissolve the suppositories. I came up with the idea of crushing and dissolving Dulcolax tablets in hot water and using a children's enema bottle to administer them directly. It works very well.

We do not think Ray can even run a fever now. If he can, it is very low grade. In the early years after his accident, he could run a fever; so this has changed. A hot summer day presents another problem. Then his body temperature will quickly go above 100 degrees F. Cold temperatures outside are difficult, too. Ray cannot shiver to warm himself. Shivering is the most efficient way for your body to warm itself, but most quadriplegics cannot shiver.

After six of these seven cases of pneumonia, we still need some additional help to prevent pneumonia. Learning about his sensitivity to oxygen is a tremendous help in treating him. Helping him regulate his body temperature should be helping also.

These cases of pneumonia are all pseudomonas pneumonia. His pseudomonas pneumonia is sensitive to tobramycin. Doctors sometimes prescribe Tobramycin breathing treatments as a preventative. The normal treatment is 28 days on then 28 days off on a continual basis. The doctors decide to prescribe this.

Another method of preventing pneumonia is applying percussion therapy daily to the chest to loosen mucus and help clear it from the lungs. We are using percussion therapy at home and in the hospital. We start by using a cupped hand on the back of his chest. Later we are able to get a hand-held percussion machine to use at home. These methods do not effectively clear his lungs. The doctor then prescribes a chest percussion wrap. An air pump drives the chest percussion wrap vibrating the chest. Cystic fibrosis patients often use this machine. The system is called a Smart vest.

After the six cases of pneumonia, Ray goes home with tobramycin and the chest percussion machine. We do 28 days of tobramycin breathing treatments and use the chest percussion machine daily. Two weeks into his 28 days off tobramycin, Ray goes to the hospital again with hypothermia and pseudomonas pneumonia. This is certainly disappointing. We work to improve what we are doing.

We want to be sure that we are using the percussion device in the best way for Ray. With the help of the hospital, we are able to get the manufacturer to send a trainer to our house when Ray goes home. She is able to train us how to better use the device. The manufacturer also reprograms our machine to work better for Ray. Now we feel more confident in using the machine.

His primary care doctor suggests changing his tobramycin prescription to seven days on then seven days off. I ask his pulmonary doctor for his opinion. He says seven on, seven off has never been tested, but it makes sense to try it.

So on February 23, 2011, we go home with the new prescription for tobramycin, new programming and training on the chest percussion, and more determination to keep his body temperature up. Ray has now been free of pneumonia for over six years. We are thankful and amazed at this result.

Since he has been free from pneumonia for so long, his doctor thinks he might not need the tobramycin now. We discontinue tobramycin on a trial basis in June of 2017. After five months, he continues to be stable; so we hope we can permanently discontinue tobramycin. We continually reevaluate his medicines at doctor appointments. Like all of us, his needs for medicines change over time.

Lesson Learned: Our knowledge of Ray is essential to help medical professionals treat him. Our knowledge helps doctors select the best treatments.

Tip: Repeated hospitalizations need reviewing. Medicare sometimes penalizes hospitals if they readmit a patient for the same diagnosis shortly after discharging them. Changes in treatment may be necessary to prevent chronic problems.

15 SEIZURES

1 Peter 5:7 Cast all your anxiety on him because he cares for you.

Seizures are very common after a traumatic brain injury, but this is not an issue with Ray for nine years. October 17, 2009, Ray starts having full body movement seizures about 5 minutes apart. We call 911. The paramedics transport him to the ER. His chest x-ray shows pneumonia. The hospital admits him to treat the pneumonia and seizures.

He is not on any seizure medication at this time. Nothing they try in the ER stops the seizures. Eventually they completely sedate him with propofol, intubate him, and put him on a respirator. In ICU, they try various seizure medications. With each attempt, they taper off the propofol to see if the seizures return. It takes several attempts before they successfully stop the seizures.

We always ask the doctors questions so we can have a better understanding. Sometimes we ask why he is getting a certain treatment or medication. Since seizures are new to us, we have more questions than usual. In this case, one of his neurologists is offended because he thinks we do not trust him. He even stops coming to Ray's room. He just reads his chart and writes orders without seeing Ray or talking to us. This is an unfortunate misunderstanding. It is good that he alternates with another neurologist who keeps us informed.

The pneumonia probably triggers the seizures, but we do not understand much about his seizures yet. We learn by experience that illness or pain triggers his seizures. Typical causes are pneumonia, kidney stones, and urinary tract infections.

Over the next four years, he has several illnesses and seizures. Sometimes the seizure medications are changed to stop his seizures. He is now on a good mix of medications for controlling his seizures.

Tip: You need to choose doctors that communicate well with you, or you should feel free to ask for another physician.

16 RAY IS JUST DIFFERENT

This episode begins when Ray goes into the hospital with pneumonia. Hospitalization is always necessary because IV antibiotics are required to treat him. They put in a PICC line to administer the antibiotics. This is a long catheter inserted through a vein in the arm.

Ray is on a monitor that displays heart rate, blood oxygen, respiration and blood pressure on a screen by his bed. The monitor has audio and visual alarms, which trigger when one of the measurements goes out of the normal range. They always monitor him when he has pneumonia. We always watch the monitor closely and are familiar with it. This is very useful because we can see when he begins to trend toward an unsafe range.

Ray begins to have several incidences when his heart rate begins to "brady down" (bradycardia) into the 20's. A heart rate below 50 triggers the monitor alarms. Below 30 is dangerous. When Ray has pneumonia, his heart rate is usually between 80 and 100. When he brady's down, the nurse runs to get a stimulant for his heart to get the rate back to normal. After a few brady down incidents, his nurse begins to carry a syringe of the stimulant in her pocket.

A cardiologist consults on this problem. He concludes that Ray probably does this on a regular basis even at home. He says we just are not aware of it because he is not on a monitor at home. He says they can stimulate his heart, but it should return to normal on its own. Ray has been in the hospital on a monitor three times in the past year. We have watched his monitor for five or six weeks total during these hospital stays. We have never seen a brady down before, so we are highly skeptical of this diagnosis.

When Ray is in the hospital, I spend the nights with him. In the morning, Lawana relieves me for the day. After two days of this brady down situation, I am trying to think of anything that is different about this hospital stay. As I am driving home, it occurs to me that most, maybe all, of the brady down incidents occur right after they push saline or medicine in one of the PICC ports with a syringe. He has not had any trouble with a PICC in the past so I wonder if the PICC is too close to his heart. Then maybe the push is affecting a valve or something else in his heart. So I pull into a parking lot and call my wife. I explain my theory and ask her to find a doctor to see if they can pull back the PICC a little bit from his heart.

She finds his pulmonary doctor and explains the theory. He sees the possibility and requests pulling back the PICC. He meets resistance to this request. They tell him a PICC cannot cause this problem. He pushes back. He says he does not care. Ray is different in everything else, so he might be different in this also. Pull it back anyway. They pull it back. It works – he does not brady down any more. You have to appreciate a doctor who will listen and go to bat for you.

One time a nurse wants to argue with Lawana about not giving Ray oxygen. She states, "Honey, you don't understand medical things." Lawana replies, "No, you don't understand Ray."

Sometimes doctors ask us if we have had medical training; and we tell them, "No. We have had on the job training."

Lesson Learned: Our observations are vital. Do not be afraid to discuss unusual ideas with your doctor. You may see something the doctors are missing.

17 COMMUNICATION BREAKTHROUGH

For several years, we take Ray to the Mary K. Chapman speech clinic at the University of Tulsa. Since Ray is an alumnus (MBA 1990), he gets a discounted rate to receive speech therapy from students. We have tried several devices and communication techniques.

As mentioned before, we think Ray can read words on a TV screen. One semester we concentrate on confirming Ray can read and spell. We put two small words on a board and ask Ray to look at the correct spelling. We also put short sentences on the board to test his ability to read. He is unable to respond every session, but he is able to do it often enough to convince us he can read and spell.

One of the professors suggests we go to the ISAAC 2012 in Pittsburgh, PA. ISAAC is the International Society for Augmentative and Alternative Communication. Their goal is to create awareness about how AAC can help individuals without speech. We take Ray specifically to learn about brain control interface (BCI) research. We know BCI is still in the research phase. We think Ray might be able to participate in research testing of a BCI device.

While we are there, we look at several other devices – eye gaze, switches, and minimum movement devices. The devices do not work for Ray. It is too early in the research phase for Ray to participate in BCI device trial. We do not meet any of our goals to find a device.

However, one evening at a social event, we are roaming around talking to various people about Ray and communication. An official in NIH (National Institutes of Health) comes up to Ray and begins to talk with him. She wants him to respond with his eyes. We explain he cannot communicate with his eyes. She politely tells us she is talking to Ray, so we back off and watch. She asks Ray to close his eyes and hold them closed. To our surprise, he does it. To this day, we use this as Ray's "yes". Previously Ray cannot hold his eyes closed, but this time he can do it. It just took 12 years for him to recover this ability. Even now he cannot always close his eyes, but he can do it often enough to be useful. This is a major communication breakthrough.

Communication is always our long-range goal for Ray. Further development of eye control is probably the best outcome. Technology wise, brain control interface may be a possibility in the future.

Lesson learned: We learn to be open to help from an unusual source. Just because past attempts fail, we should not be afraid to try again at a future time.

18 SOMETIMES EVERYTHING GOES WRONG

Deuteronomy 31:6 Be strong and courageous. Do not be afraid or terrified because of them, for the LORD your God goes with you; he will never leave you nor forsake you.

Saturday, April 13, 2013, 9:09 a.m. Ray has a five-minute seizure and his right pupil dilates. I call his neurologist and get him immediately on the phone. He doubles one of his three seizure medications. Since he gets everything by PEG tube (a tube directly into his stomach), we are able to give him the increased dose immediately.

9:41 a.m.: He has a six- minute seizure. 10:15 a.m.: He has a five-minute seizure. 10:24 a.m.: He has another five-minute seizure. We call 911 for transport to ER. He has several seizures in ER.

The ER doctor orders a CT scan of the brain, a chest x-ray, blood test, and urine test. All of these tests are fine – not even any blood in the urine. We skip his noon feeding because he has high residuals in his stomach. (We always test his stomach with a feeding syringe to make sure it is empty before we feed him.) By now, his seizures have stopped, so they release him to go home.

At 5:30 p.m., after we are home, we check his stomach for residuals. He still has 240 ml fluid in his stomach. At 6:25 p.m., he still has the 240 ml residual. We skip his evening meal. This time we discard the residuals to empty his stomach and give it a break. At 8 p.m., we give him 100 ml water to test his stomach. At 9:40 p.m., he has 120 ml residuals. We discard it. Even though his stomach is not working yet, he needs his seizure medications; so we give him his medications with 200 ml water hoping he will absorb these. We all go to bed.

Sunday, 2:30 a.m. He has no residuals, so I am able to give him some water. We keep him home Sunday. Stomach residuals are higher than normal Sunday, but they are low enough for us to feed him all of his meals. His urine output is low and his weight is up 3 lbs. from Friday even though he missed two meals Saturday. He is probably retaining water.

Monday: He is up two more pounds. His urine output continues to be low. He has a history of kidney stones, so we begin to think he is trying to pass a stone. We make appointments with his neurologist and his urologist. Stomach residuals continue to be a problem but he manages to get all three meals. We decide not to take him back to the ER now because we think they will just give him pain medication if it is a kidney stone. This turns out to be a mistake on our part.

Tuesday: Urine output is nearly normal. His weight is up one more pound. We see his neurologist. His seizures seem to be under control, so we keep the new dose of medicine we started Saturday. He has a seizure at 9 p.m. He seems to be in pain, so we give him Tylenol.

Wednesday: Urine output is good. His weight is down one pound. Still some problems with stomach residuals. We take him to his urologist. We think they are doing a CT of the abdomen. Instead, they do a flat plate x-ray. The x-ray shows he has some kidney stones but the x-ray does not give enough detail to see the significance of his problem. Convinced he still has a problem, we are able to schedule a CT of the abdomen for Friday.

Thursday: His weight is the same as Wednesday, which is five pounds above his starting weight. Urine output is a little low. No problems with residuals.

Friday: There is visible blood in his urine. Urine output is low. He has many problems with residuals causing him to miss two meals. We discard residuals to give his stomach a break. His weight is down one lb., which is four lbs. above his starting weight. His left pupil dilates, but he has no seizures. We take him to his urologist's lab for the CT of the abdomen as scheduled. His urologist will be out of the office Monday, so we will not get the results until Tuesday. In retrospect, we should have taken him to the ER when we saw blood in his urine.

Saturday, Sunday, and Monday: Continued blood in urine, obvious pain – giving him Tylenol. His weight is now seven pounds above his starting weight. His heart rate is 101. It is usually around 70. High heart rate is a main indicator of a problem for Ray. Monday we take Ray and a urine sample to his primary care physician but we are unable to get the CT results.

Tuesday: His heart rate continues high at 103. He passes a 1.5 mm kidney stone and four smaller ones. The nurse for his urologist calls with the CT results. He has a 6.4 mm stone obstruction in the left kidney. It is too large to pass. We take him to the ER where he is admitted to have the stone removed surgically.

We settle into his hospital room. The nurse asks for his medication list and makes a copy of it. It is mid-afternoon Tuesday. His 6 p.m. Prevacid does not show up. I call the nurses desk and ask for it, but it never comes. 7 p.m. is nurse shift change. At 7 p.m., it is time to feed him. Missing one dose of Prevacid is not critical, so I go ahead and feed him (I always bring his medical food from home because the hospital never has it.).

Soon the new nurse comes to check on Ray. I tell her his 6 p.m. medication never came. I also tell her he is due two breathing treatments now and he will need his 10 p.m. medications. At 10 p.m., he has not received either breathing treatment or any medications. So I check with the nurse.

She says the doctor did not order any medications because he is having surgery in the morning. Now his medications are mainly seizure medications, so I know something is wrong. I tell her I am coming to the desk to read the doctor's order myself. When I get to the desk, she and a male nurse are reading the doctor's orders. She says the doctor ordered "home meds." Therefore, I ask, "Does that mean I should have brought his medications from home?" She says, "It means he should get the same medications he would get at home. But no medications were entered into the system." I explain, rather forcefully, that he is late now, and he may have seizures if we do not get them soon. In addition, I remind her he is not to have anything by mouth after midnight.

At 11:20 p.m., she brings some medications but they are wrong. I always check his medications because I have seen many mistakes like this. Due to a hospital "safeguard" that I have never understood, the pharmacy sends the medications from his previous hospitalization even though the nurse has entered the current list. I reject the ones that are wrong and ask them to send the pharmacist on the floor to Ray's room. He does not come to the room, but he calls me. I explain Ray needs his current medications now. At 11:40 p.m., the nurse brings the correct medications to the room. All of this reminds me how important it is for us to know his medications, including any new medications ordered in the hospital. It is very important for one of us to be with him 24 hours per day to make sure he gets the correct medications and treatments.

Let me talk about our experiences with liquid medications in the hospital. At home, we generally crush tablets and dissolve them in water to go down Ray's PEG tube. We prefer tablets to liquid medication because the tablets are premeasured. As a doctor recently told me, "If you use liquid medications, it will be wrong sometime. You are depending on measuring it correctly. You are also depending on someone mixing the correct concentration. Mistakes will happen."

When you pick up a liquid medication from a retail pharmacy, the label tells you the volume (milliliters, ounces, or teaspoons) to take. They calculate this based on the concentration of the solution. Going back to the statement the doctor made about liquid medications, if the pharmacy uses the wrong concentration or if you measure it incorrectly, then you do not get the correct dose.

Since Ray gets his oral medications though his PEG tube, our hospital pharmacy changes his prescriptions to liquid solutions if liquid is available. In our experience, they do not ask anybody, they just do it. During Ray's most recent hospitalization, the hospital pharmacy furnished the liquid medications in premeasured doses. In the past, each nurse had to calculate the volume. The new procedure is a huge improvement because it eliminates the possibility of the nurse calculating or measuring the volume incorrectly.

We also need to inform the anesthesiologist, surgeon, and recovery room attendants about his sensitivity to oxygen. For Ray, they will only give him oxygen during the surgery while a respirator controls his breathing. This is acceptable because the respirator will make sure he breathes enough to expel his carbon dioxide. The recovery room nurses go to our church, so we are able to coordinate with them in advance. They normally use oxygen in recovery just to make it easier to breathe, but they will not give Ray any oxygen.

Wednesday: The surgery is delayed because his medicine from the pharmacy arrives late. It arrives late because, at the last minute, the pharmacy decides to substitute a liquid medicine instead of crushing a tablet. After this delay, surgery and recovery go well. He spends the night in the hospital and goes home Thursday.

Lesson Learned: Being an active advocate is essential. We never leave Ray by himself in the hospital. One of us is always there with him.

Tip: Try to understand all medications and what the medications treat. Too many times patients just take medications without understanding the purpose of the medications.

19 HOUSING

When Ray comes to live with us, we remodel his old bedroom, making it accessible. An old friend, Herman Johnson, did some previous work on our house. Herman, our minister at another congregation, is a life-long acquaintance of Ray. He and Bill Ellis, another church friend, donate their time and remodel the bedroom to fit Ray's new situation.

We take out the closet so the new bathroom can be close to existing plumbing. Ray's children really enjoy participating in the demolition. They have a ball hammering down the walls. Herman and Bill install a toilet, sink and roll-in shower. They build a new closet and a window seat that provides storage. There is already a large bookcase unit with a desktop and drawers in the room. A three-foot wide bedroom door provides wheelchair access. Vinyl flooring replaces the old carpeting.

While we remodel the room, we use another bedroom for Ray. His wheelchair will not go through the door, so we transfer him to the patient lift in the living room and roll it down the hallway into the bedroom. It takes about three months for the remodeling to be finished.

One morning, Lawana sees that Ray is crying. She tells Herman. He comes and speaks with Ray for a long time. Herman is a talented counselor who spends time helping others even after leaving the ministry. Herman and Bill exercise Ray weekly until their own ill health prevents them.

We expect Ray to outlive us, so future care for him is a concern. We hope someone will care for him at home, as we have. Since our remodeled home is on a rural acreage, we doubt anyone will want to take care of Ray and the acreage. While we like the extra space, we will not be able to maintain this property forever.

In 2006, we decide to build an accessible home on a regular city lot. I design a single story floor plan, which meets our unique needs. We select a housing addition and a builder. The builder completes the house plan and begins construction late in 2006.

March 2007, we move into our new home. It has ten-foot ceilings with nine-foot tall garage doors. The garage doors are tall enough for Ray's wheelchair van. We put a four-foot wide door in line with the van lift so we can roll Ray into the entry hall from the van while the van is in the garage. This keeps Ray out of the weather.

Our interior doors are three-foot wide for wheelchair access. The bedrooms open off a large family room, so we do not have a bedroom hall to navigate. Ray's bedroom, the family room, and entry hall have tile floors to make it easier to roll the wheelchair. Ray's bedroom is extra-large. It includes a large roll-in shower, toilet, cabinets, and a single bowl kitchen sink. His PT table is in this room also. The closet is a walk-in closet with extra shelves for storage. The hospital bed for Ray and a couch for us are in the room. A TV on the wall is visible from his bed, the PT table, and the couch.

Tip: If you have accessibility needs, it may be better to modify your current home first. After you use it for a while, you will have a better idea of your needs should you decide build or make other changes.

In 2007, we built a new home with features to help us care for Ray easier. This is the work area in his room. You can also see his bed. To the left is the toilet.

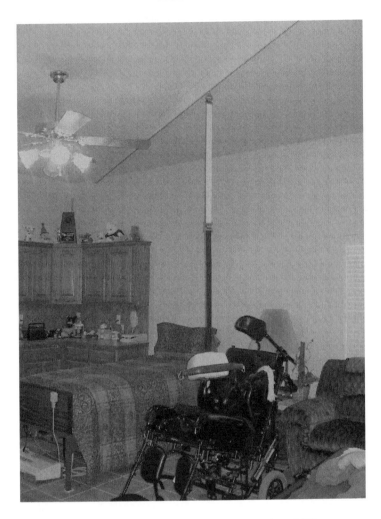

This is his room showing the overhead lift.

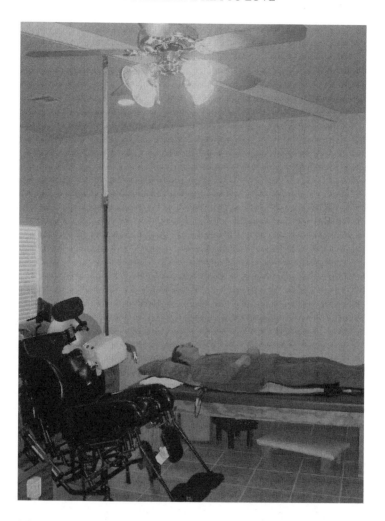

This is Ray laying on the PT table for a workout. You can also see the overhead lift and the position of the wheelchair.

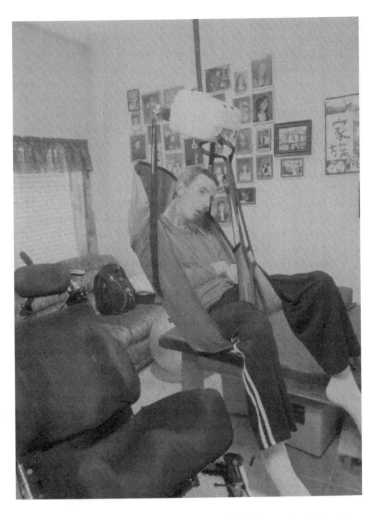

Transferring Ray with the overhead lift from the PT table to his wheelchair.

The roll-in shower and shower chair in his room. The shower controls are on the end so we can reach them easily.

We have a 4-foot wide door in the entry hall that lines up with the wheelchair lift in Ray's van so we can load and unload him out of the weather.

20 TYPICAL DAY AND ROUTINE CARE

Psalm 68:19 Praise be to the Lord, to God our Savior, who daily bears our burdens.

The original ten days of training in daily care and therapy got us off to a good start. Since then, we have been able to refine his care with guidance from doctors, therapists, nurses, nurse techs, and college professors. These opportunities have come from hospitalizations, inpatient and outpatient services, working with local colleges and universities, and attending a couple of conferences, in addition to regular medical appointments. Occasionally, we are able to share our experiences with medical personnel.

We have an overhead lift for transferring Ray between his home hospital bed, PT table, and either his regular custom wheelchair or his shower wheelchair. We also have a nebulizer, suction machine, and chest percussion machine.

6:30 a.m.: We shift Ray in his bed and give him medicine. We give all oral medicines and food through his PEG tube with water for flushing.

7:15 a.m.: He gets a breathing treatment, and medical food (formula

9 a.m.: We give him a sponge bath in bed with mouth care. For Ray's mouth care we brush his teeth with a disposable oral swab (Dentip) coated with dentifrice and then squeeze some of the solution onto his toothbrush and brush his teeth again. We use a tongue brush (Tung) to scrape the roof of his mouth. It is surprising how much gunk can accumulate there. Three days a week, we shampoo his hair. He gets his seizure medications. His eyes are very dry because he does not blink enough, so we put eye gel in his eyes. Occasionally, he also needs allergy eye drops. We dress him in clothes that are one size too large because they are easier to get on him. We have also found that stretchy clothes smooth out more easily to prevent wrinkles. Since Ray does not move, wrinkles can cause pressure sore problems.

10 a.m.: A regular volunteer helps me stretch Ray on the PT table.

10:45 a.m.: We transfer him to his wheelchair and put on his chest percussion wrap. We roll him into the family room to watch TV while the percussion machine runs. We give him 30 minutes of chest percussion. When it is finished, we remove the chest wrap. He continues to watch TV for the day. When we are not sure what he wants to watch, we give him choices and ask him to close his eyes to answer.

12 p.m.: We shift Ray in his wheelchair for pressure relief. We shift him hourly throughout the day. We give him a breathing treatment and his medical food.

3 p.m.: We put eye gel in his eyes and give him cranberry juice, lemon juice and a laxative. The lemon juice is a preventative for kidney stones. He still gets stones but not as often.

4:30 p.m.: We give him 30 minutes of chest percussion.

5 p.m. (approximate time – actual time varies with the volunteer's availability): A regular volunteer stretches Ray on the PT table. At 5 p.m. I usually help transfer him to the table and back to the chair.

7 p.m.: We give him a breathing treatment and his medical food.

9 p.m.: We put Ray to bed, give him medicines and eye gel. We use pillows under his elbows for pressure relief and behind his back for positioning.

2:30 a.m.: I turn him in bed; give him eye gel and lemon juice. I remove the back pillows and place a pillow on the left side of his head to keep it aligned.

There are a few regular differences in the daily routine. Monday, Wednesday and Friday we give a suppository at 7:15 a.m. for bowel movement management. On Saturday, we put him in his shower wheelchair and roll him into the roll-in shower for a shower and shampoo. We do not use volunteers on Saturday. We have a part-time employee who bathes him two days a week. On Sunday, he does not get chest percussion and only gets one workout on the PT table so we can all go to church at 9 a.m. and 5 p.m. On Wednesday nights, we attend the 7 p.m. church service.

Lesson Learned: Our initial training is very helpful. We are able to improve by learning "on the job" and visiting with healthcare professionals. I am pleased to be able to use medical training from my military service.

21 MEDICAL CARE

Primary Care: Ray has a physical examination annually and follow-up appointments every six months with his primary care physician. This is the best opportunity to discuss and check his overall health. We review what all the specialists are doing for Ray. Lab tests are reviewed which can lead to a discussion of all his medications and possible interactions or side effects. We always take a written list of questions for the doctor that generate discussion. We are always looking at medicine adjustments or elimination. Frequently the doctor needs to call one of Ray's specialists with a question or a suggestion. Sometimes we need a referral to evaluate a treatment, equipment or therapy that may be beneficial. We are blessed to have a primary care physician whom we have known through church in the past.

Vision: Annual eye examination is necessary to check for glaucoma and dry eyes. Ray has dry eyes because he does not blink enough to keep them lubricated. This is particularly dangerous for the corneas because their health is dependent on lubricating tears. Ray has had to have crystals removed manually from his corneas due to the dryness. Dry eyes are particularly difficult to treat. His family history has several cases of glaucoma (his mother has glaucoma and both grandmothers had glaucoma).

Neurologist: Ray has semiannual appointments with his neurologist for seizure control. He has not had seizures recently so we are concentrating on gradual seizure medication adjustments to minimize long-term side effects. Secondarily, we also look at the costs of the medications. The doctors learn more about these medications with time. I am sure new medications will become available that we may consider.

Urologist: Ray has an annual ultrasound examination and appointment with his urologist monitoring his kidney stones. Kidney stones have only become a problem in recent years. As I understand it, Ray is susceptible to kidney stones because he is a quadriplegic. Quadriplegics do not have load bearing on their bones to keep them strong; so his bones are gradually losing density, which is a loss of calcium. This extra calcium passes through the kidneys. Extra calcium means extra danger of kidney stones. We give him lemon juice twice a day to help reduce the possibility of stones. We also have discontinued one medication known for increasing the possibility of kidney stones. He does not have osteoporosis yet, but his bones are noticeably less dense on x-rays now. We are also trying some other medication changes to minimize the loss of bone density.

E. N. T.: Earwax build up is a problem for Ray, so he sees an ear specialist regularly. I have this problem also, so it may not be related to his injury. I think the buildup in one of his ears is worse due to his head being tilted to the same side all of the time, so gravity is probably complicating this.

Dental: We schedule dental cleaning and examinations every six months. Dental care is difficult because they cannot spray water in Ray's mouth due to his swallowing difficulties. They use sponges instead of water for cleanup. Our dental office is particularly patient and careful with him. It is hard to get his wheelchair in position so they can use their equipment, but we manage. Once they had to refer him to a specialist to have a broken tooth pulled because it had broken down into the gum. He has another broken tooth that is not decaying or causing gum problems, so we leave it alone.

Health Issues: We are continually aware of the two main health risks for Ray. His biggest risk is pneumonia. We use a fingertip pulse-ox to monitor his oxygen and his pulse. Both of these measurements are important. We use a temporal thermometer for his body temperature. We carry both of these everywhere. The chest percussion machine is a great preventative measure. The sound of his breathing and coughing are good indicators of the beginning of respiratory problems.

The next biggest risk is his skin. His custom seating and the alternating pressure mattress are essential equipment for prevention of pressure sores. His private insurance provided his first alternating pressure air mattress because he had a bad pressure sore. We have been so successful at skin care that he seldom gets a pressure sore. When he does, it is minor. Most insurance will only provide an alternating pressure air mattress when you have a serious pressure sore. Then it is only rented until the sore is healed. Since we now use the special mattresses for prevention, we have to buy them ourselves. Fortunately, we can buy an inexpensive (about $600) one online. They only last a few years, so this is a regular expense but well worth it.

I think Ray's health is complicated. On one hand, he is slowly recovering and improving in some areas. Examples of this are screaming, eye closing for communication, and reduction in spasticity eliminating the need of the baclofen pump. Other factors may be deteriorating: such as the development of seizure problems, losing the ability to run a fever, and possibly his oxygen sensitivity. The long-term toll of being a quadriplegic and generally aging (Ray is 51 now.) are causing bone density deterioration and kidney stones. Long-term side effects of medications will take a toll. Since Ray was only 34 when he was injured, he may be on some medications much longer than most people. Ray's inability to explain symptoms adds another level of complication because we may not even know he is sick until it is serious enough to create a seizure, high heart rate, or other obvious measurable sign.

Some other health issues over the years include a blood clot in the calf of his right leg in 2001. Probably he is more at risk since he is a quadriplegic. We started giving him a low dose aspirin daily to thin his blood as a preventative.

Then in 2007, he has a bad lower GI bleed. We almost lose him. As the doctor and I are running to ICU, he asks me if he should resuscitate Ray if necessary. Without hesitation, I answer "yes." You never want to face this decision, but knowing Ray is fully cognitive makes me comfortable with this decision. They give him four units of blood because he lost so much blood they cannot detect his blood pressure. Fortunately, the bleeding stops on its own. We discontinue the aspirin and never restart it. We just decide a GI bleed is a bigger risk than a blood clot.

In 2007, he has a heart ablation to burn out an extra electrical circuit in his heart that is causing his heart to race. He was born with this extra circuit but it did not cause any trouble until he was in his 40s. When we become aware of this problem, I buy a heart rate chest band from a sporting goods store to monitor his heart rate. With this monitor, we are able to detect the heart race episodes. Since Ray cannot tell us when he is having difficulty, the monitor is very useful. This ablation eliminates the heart race problem.

Communication is always our long-range goal for Ray. Further development of eye control is probably the best outcome. Technology wise, brain control interface may be a possibility in the future.

Tip: Do not assume your dentist, or other provider, cannot accommodate your disability without asking them.

22 HIS CHILDREN

Psalm 127:3 Children are a heritage from the Lord, offspring a reward from him.

Two months before Ray's accident, Ray and Shannon move to a new house eight miles from our house. We enjoy being close enough to help with their children. After several years, Shannon does remarry but she continues to live in the same house until the youngest one goes away to college. This way she provides stability for the children. They have a stable neighborhood, school, and church environment. In 2007 we are able to build our new home just two miles from Shannon. This is pleasing to Shannon and us because it makes transportation between the houses even easier. Since we now live in their school district, they can spend nights at our house and still ride the school bus to and from school.

When Ray has his accident, Travis is eight years old, Nicole is six, and Raychel is four. He is very involved in his children's lives. Ray coaches Travis' baseball team and is to take him to his first basketball practice the night of the accident. He always has time to play with them and teach them how to throw a ball or any other activity or skill. He is a real "hands on" dad.

When Ray begins to live with us, we want Ray and his children to continue to have a strong relationship. Shannon is very willing for the children to spend nearly every weekend with us and to go to church with us on Sundays and Wednesday nights. We always keep Ray involved in their school and church activities. He goes to back-to-school nights, band concerts, chorus programs, athletic games, award assemblies and various other events. We make several overnight trips to see Travis play ultimate Frisbee tournaments with the Harding team. In many instances, we act for Ray in the role of parent instead of grandparent.

The old saying "It takes a village to raise a child." is especially true in the case of Ray's children. Our church family is such a big influence on them. Travis participates in the Boy Scout troop meeting at our church building until he is 18 years old. He benefits from the camping activities and other exposure to Christian men. In 2010, he is able to go on a medical mission trip to Guyana. One summer, Nicole spends six weeks in Japan on a mission effort teaching English and the Bible. As youth, they especially enjoy summer camp and youth activities. Travis and Nicole are counselors during our church camp week one summer. Nicole and Raychel work in our day camp for neighborhood children several summers. God blessed me to baptize all three of them.

We make several road trips with Ray and his children during summer vacation. The longest trips are to Yellowstone, Mount Rushmore and the Great Lakes. We make shorter trips to Missouri, Arkansas, and Texas and around Oklahoma.

After high school, Ray's children all attend Ray's alma mater Harding University in Searcy, Arkansas. Nicole graduates from Harding with honors. She is a high school mathematics teacher. She is married to Nathaniel Michael, a minister. Ray is able to "walk" her down the aisle with me pushing his wheelchair. In 2017, Nicole gives birth to a little girl they name Thea Wren. Ray is now a grandfather and we are great grandparents.

Travis is living in Searcy. He is attending Harding majoring accounting. Raychel attends Harding for two years before transferring to Oklahoma State University. She is majoring in Spanish.

All three children regularly visit their dad and us. Saturday night dinner followed by games is a tradition. Holidays are important times for us to be together. One Christmas, we hold our gift exchange in Ray's hospital room with everyone dressed in isolation gowns because of Ray's history of MRSA. As we age, they will begin to take responsibility for their dad's care and financial affairs.

Lesson Learned: Family is a blessing from God no matter what your circumstances. When in a difficult situation, it is even more important to keep communication open and keep those bonds strong.

Tip: Children need stability.

Nicole being silly with her dad

Summer vacation to Yellowstone in 2006

Travis, Nicole and Raychel on Independence Rock in Wyoming in 2006

Ray and Travis at the new Busch stadium for a Cardinals baseball game in 2007. I took Ray to the first aid room twice to cool him because it was too hot for him.

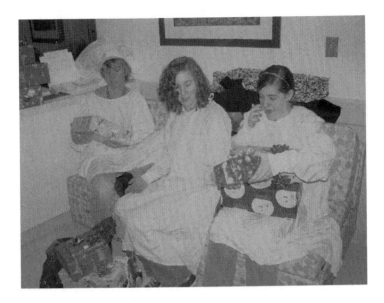

In 2010 Ray's children, Travis, Nicole and Raychel opened their Christmas presents in Ray's hospital room. We had to wear isolation gowns in his room. Sometimes you just have to go with the flow.

Nathaniel, Nicole, Travis and Raychel at Christmas in 2013.

Thea Wren Michael at 4 weeks old

23 RAY MADE GOOD FRIENDS

Proverbs 17:17 "A friend loves at all times".

Ray made friends everywhere – neighborhood, school, church, college and work. He still enjoys being with his friends. He kept renewing and nurturing those friendships before the accident. This has paid off many times over. They help in many ways, but most of all Ray lights up when he sees them. Ray's friends have been there for him. They always say Ray would have been the first to be there for them.

Many of Ray's friends have also connected with Ray's children. I think it encourages them. Two of his local friends, Roger Roth and Rich Conrad, exercise him every week so they stay very current on Ray and his children. Some of his Harding friends have helped fund their college education. One has been able to fund most of the tuition. I think they will all finish without debt, which is amazing in today's world.

We take Ray to homecoming at Harding every year so he keeps renewing friendships. Dave Finley and Rick Butler always catch up with us at homecoming. They were members of Kappa Tau Omega social club at Harding with Ray. They have close relationships with Ray's children and keep other Harding alumni up-to-date on Ray. Almost every year we meet someone new who remembers Ray from his college years. Now some administrators at Harding were students with Ray. It is common for one of Ray's children to find they are meeting with an administrator who knows their father.

When Ray turned 40 years old, some of his friends organized a surprise birthday party for him. About 20 traveled from several states, brought gifts and spent the day reminiscing. They included Ray's children in part of the day. Then they paid us to take his children bowling so they could share more freely with Ray.

Sadly, it is too emotional for some of Ray's friends to be with him. They say it is too painful to see him the way he is after his being such an active fun-loving individual. We are thankful to those who have been able to keep a relationship with him through the years.

Lesson Learned: We became acquainted with Ray's friends and nurtured those relationships. They help us in many ways and really boost his quality of life.

Harding homecoming 2005 with college classmates

Some college classmates surprise Ray with a party on his 40th birthday at our house in 2006.

Ray with the college friends who surprise him

The party moved from our house to another house. Then these high school classmates joined the party.

24 OTHER FAMILY MEMBERS

We balance our responsibilities to Ray with those to other family members. My parents and Lawana's father were already deceased by the time of Ray's accident. Lawana's mother, Bessie, and nephew, Danny, lived together after her dad passed away in 1998. Her sister, Joyce, moved in with Bessie about 2004 and died in 2005. Danny had to have a leg amputated for cancer in 2005. Lawana spent ten days in Oklahoma City staying with him for the surgery. We presented quite a sight on Mother's Day that year when we had to manipulate three wheelchairs through the doors of a restaurant. When Danny died in 2006, Bessie came to live with us. She passed away in September of 2007, but, for a while, we were caring for two disabled persons.

I have a brother, David, who lives with his family in Duncan, Oklahoma, and a sister, Kay, who lives in Hulbert, OK. We try to visit with them when we can.

Our daughter, Regina, has three daughters, Sarah, Hannah, and Becky. We try to be attentive grandparents to these girls. Holidays have always been important. We have been able to travel to spend them with Regina's family when it was necessary. Regina and Becky lived with us for three years and have now moved to their own house. Sarah graduated from Harding in December of 2016. Hannah recently graduated from high school.

Lesson Learned: We try to keep our close family relationships and not neglect other family members.

Our daughter, Regina, and her daughters, Becky, Hannah and Sarah, at Christmas in 2015.

25 THE INNOCENCE OF LITTLE CHILDREN

Matthew 18:3 And he said: "Truly I tell you, unless you change and become like little children, you will never enter the kingdom of heaven.

At our church, we dismiss preschool children to their Bible Hour before the Sunday morning sermon. This morning three girls were passing by Ray. When they got to Ray, they stopped to greet him. They waved their hands to get Ray's attention, smiled and said "Hi." I could not see Ray's eyes, but he usually makes eye contact and closes his eyes to respond to them. Everyone behind them stopped and smiled while they waited until the girls finished. This brought tears to my eyes to see them interact with Ray.

Little children are refreshingly direct. One day, before Ray could respond by closing his eyes, I remember noticing a little girl standing in front of Ray looking at him. She asked, "What happened to him?" I said he was in an automobile accident. She asked, "Can he talk?" I said no but he can smile. She said to Ray, "Smile". I explained he could only smile at something funny. She immediately put her thumbs in her ears and made a funny face. Ray did not smile. I could not get Ray to smile for her either, but I think these conversations are good for all of us — especially for the children.

I have seen young mothers explain to their little ones who are staring at Ray that he has an "owie" and cannot walk. His wheelchair fascinates small children.

Many of the children at our congregation are well aware of Ray and show their interest in him by writing notes, drawing pictures, and speaking to him. Teachers in the preschool and primary departments have told us that the little children frequently mention Ray in their prayers.

Tip: Little children can give you an emotional lift.

26 INSURANCE

Ray was working for Hilti as a purchasing specialist at the time of the accident (December 2000). He had group medical insurance and their standard long-term disability insurance. Additionally, he purchased a group accidental death and dismemberment (AD&D), and a group life insurance policy. This was a good choice of policies for this circumstance.

Hilti put him on short-term disability for 3 months. This provided full salary. He then went on long-term disability (LTD). LTD pay was a significant reduction in pay. He went on Social Security disability in June 2001. When he went on Social Security, his LTD benefit reduced to the minimum because his Social Security benefit was more than his LTD.

Ray remained on Hilti's group medical insurance until June 2002. I believe Hilti picked up the premiums when he went on LTD. Ray was not eligible for Medicare until June 2003. To fill the gap between group insurance and Medicare we were able to buy COBRA, a federal program which mandates insurance continuance. When Ray went on Medicare, we bought a Medicare supplement insurance policy. At the time he went on Medicare, prescription drug coverage was not available so we had to pay full price for his prescriptions until Part D policies became available.

The AD&D policy paid the full benefit to Ray because he lost the use of all four limbs. The life insurance has a Waiver of Premium benefit for disability. Both LTD and the life insurance Waiver of Premium benefit require annual proof of disability. The policies require a physician's statement each year. After a few years, it became obvious that Ray is disabled for life. The physician's statement became a drudgery for the doctor and us. I explained this to both companies. They both agreed they would waive the annual physician's statement if his doctor would write a letter of explanation. Now they are not requiring annual physician's statements, but they reserve the right to request one. I do have to fill out a simple form for them each year.

A settlement was awarded to Ray from the accident. This was paid directly into a Special Needs Trust administered by a bank trust department for Ray's benefit. If Ray ever qualifies for Medicaid, the trust will not be considered his asset since he does not own it. It can continue to be used for Ray's benefit without affecting Medicaid.

Ray's insurance was a Health Maintenance Organization (HMO) at the time of the accident. HMOs can be difficult because of requiring preapproval for most treatment. We were able to change to another plan in the next year. Fortunately, Lawana has worked as a medical insurance adjuster, so she could help me understand how insurance works. As you can imagine, Ray's medical costs are very expensive. It became very important to use only doctors and providers in his insurance plan. Lawana explained if we use doctors in plan, the doctors get preapproval for his medical needs. If the insurance does not pay because the doctor did not get preapproval, then Ray does not have to pay either.

It is also important to understand the policy details such as Maximum Out-of-Pocket and the unusual coverages negotiated by his employer. An unusual coverage example was no copay is required if you just have an injection at a doctor's office. Since this is not normal, the insurance adjusters missed this about half of the time. Then I would have to call the insurance company to get the claim corrected. The insurance company let Ray run over the Maximum Out-of-Pocket. We were able to get the excess charges refunded.

Sometimes providers billed us for expenses the insurance did not pay because they did not file the claim correctly. The biggest of these bills was $10,000 for some custom splints. The insurance had preapproved these but the provider did not bill the insurance company timely so the insurance did not pay. The provider's accounts payable department moved the charge to "Patient Responsibility" and billed Ray. When I called, they told me what happened. They wrote off the expense. It is important to question erroneous charges quickly.

Now that he is on Medicare, erroneous billing does not happen as often. The most common mistake is a provider filing a claim incorrectly. Sometimes a provider will make an accounting mistake that is easily resolved.

Lesson Learned: Lawana's career as a medical insurance claims adjuster has helped us navigate insurance problems.

Tip: Understand your insurances coverages. Human Resources departments will help you with their group polices. Your state insurance commissioner's office can help with Medicare supplement policy information. You may have local senior services that can help with Medicare. In catastrophic cases, private insurance companies may assign a case manager to help you.

27 ANNUAL EXPENSES

Actual expenses of Ray's care for the year 2015:

Medical supplies	$828	
Doctors	$318	
Prescriptions plus Part D premiums	$4,595	
Medical Part B + Medicare supplement premiums	$4,217	
Medical Total:		**$9,959**
Wheelchair van insurance	$935	
Van maintenance	$1,077	
Gasoline	$1,096	
Miscellaneous	$850	
Household help	$1,232	
Annual Court Report	$66	
Oklahoma tax refund	($211)	
Total of Other Expenses		**$5,079**
Total		**$15,038**

His Social Security plus Long-Term Disability pay totaled $22,223 so he has income beyond his basic expenses for travel, Christmas and birthday gifts for his children, and unusual other expenses. Frequently we have a few thousand dollars in additional expenses. Usually we draw about $3,000 from income producing investments annually to supplement his income. We are frugal so we have been able to accumulate cash reserves for large unexpected expenses.

We economize on medical supplies by purchasing most of these in bulk on-line. We probably save $400 per year compared to buying them in smaller quantities locally. We save on over the counter medications by using generics.

Every year I use Medicare.gov to select the most economical Part D plan for his current medicines. Plans change every year so it is common to change plans every year. Medicare.gov calculates your total annual cost for local pharmacies and mail order pharmacies. Oddly, for Ray it is usually $200 to $300 cheaper to use a local pharmacy. This is contrary to common belief. I think this is an unintentional quirk of the structure of the plans. If your prescription cost is low, you probably always save money using mail order.

Tip: Investigate medical insurance options. Employer group insurance plans usually have an annual open enrollment period, which may allow you to select a more appropriate plan. If options are available, review them every year.

28 RESPITE CARE

Lawana and I have generally been blessed with good health and rarely have needed to leave Ray's care to others.

Early on, while I was still working, we arranged for two women at a time from church to stay with Ray while Lawana helped her mother with doctor appointments and other errands. About twenty women signed up to help us in this way.

We were able to take a short trip to Eureka Springs, Arkansas, when my boss paid for home health care and Regina, our daughter, came to stay with Ray. Another time we spent a couple of days in Oklahoma City. Regina and her husband stayed with Ray. Otherwise, one of us has always been there to care for him.

Lawana has had three eye surgeries, carpal tunnel surgery and a colon resection in the past few years. We were able to arrange for help in bathing Ray each time. I can usually care for Ray entirely by myself if necessary. It is harder for Lawana to do this because of the strength needed. Six years ago, we decided we needed to train someone to care for Ray in case both of us were out of commission and because of Lawana's problems with arthritis in her hands. We hired Tracey Michael, Nathaniel's mother, to come in two days a week to give Ray his bath. (Nathaniel is now married to Ray's daughter Nicole.) She was working at a hospital as a nursing tech on the night shift. Recently, Tracey had to quit because her job and work schedule changed. At church we learned of a nurse in our congregation who wanted a job working only a few hours a week. We were able to hire her to take Tracey's place.

Lesson Learned: We strive to keep our life goals and give importance to our own health needs. We all need a time of recreation and recharging.

Tip: Volunteers from church may be able to help. You may have adult day care or other services available in your area.

29 THE VALUE OF SUPPORT

Philippians 1:3 I thank my God every time I remember you.
It is humbling to realize how much help and support we have needed and received. We think we are doing it all ourselves; then we realize eight, nine, or ten people have helped us this week at our house. Several people have made a special effort to talk to Ray and us at church. A child makes the effort to say "Hi" to Ray. Did we take care of this week ourselves – no, not even close.

At age 62 ½, I decided to retire to help care for Ray. When I mentioned this to my doctor, he gave me some very important advice. He said, "Don't get the idea you can do everything yourself. Keep your volunteers." Now, he knew I was going to release my volunteers and try to do it all myself. This doctor is now deceased, but he knew me well because he had been my doctor for 42 years. He knew about Ray and what was involved in his care. I guess I was prideful to think I could go it alone.

We did release the women who were sitting with Ray so Lawana could do the grocery shopping and run errands with her mother. I took his advice and kept the scheduled

volunteers who help with physical therapy. I am so glad I
kept these volunteers. I think we do not realize how much
benefit our support system is to us. These people really
keep our spirits up. Ray gets a longer and better workout
when a volunteer comes. Some volunteers workout Ray by
themselves. Additionally, he gets social interaction, which
has to be invaluable to his sense of well-being.

Not all of our support comes from people who come
to our house. Some send encouragement cards. Others
visit us when Ray is in the hospital. Fortunately, he has not
been in the hospital recently. Many visit with us and with
Ray at church. It is always encouraging when someone
visits directly with Ray. Some have given gifts to Ray's
children. One family gives us a holiday basket of
homemade goodies every year. Sometimes we receive a
basket of fruit. One older woman has given Ray two
blanket throws. People often tell us of a news report on a
communication device or some other treatment that might
help Ray. Unexpectedly, we hear our names mentioned in
a prayer. One man is able to make metal parts for us when
we need them. I know I can request help from someone
with a special talent when I need it. The smallest act of
kindness is a big blessing to us.

The help and encouragement helps us in two ways. It
helps preserve our physical strength and keeps our spirit
high. Once a month Lawana plays Bunco on a Monday
night with a group of women from church. She also plays
Mexican Train dominoes on one Thursday a month with
friends from church. I have breakfast with a men's church
group once a month. I have lunch occasionally with a
friend. All of this together helps us take care of ourselves
so we can continue our care for Ray.

Often, people, especially on cruises, approach us and
comment on Ray's condition and our being caregivers. We

are always eager to share with them the help we receive from our volunteers and our church family.

Lawana worked ten years for Bob and Wanda Phillips, some Christian friends, in their company processing medical insurance claims. In 1992, their sons, Bobby and David, were murdered. Police have never solved the crime. A few years ago, Wanda and Lawana were discussing the tragedy that each family had faced. They both agreed they could not have survived without the support each had received from Christian friends and God's Word.

We make special effort to make sure everyone knows how much we appreciate each one. At Christmas Lawana makes candy as gifts to our volunteers. We always try to express our appreciation in person. With Ray's out-of-town friends, we communicate with texts, emails, Facebook and real telephone calls.

Lesson Learned: I learned to appreciate the value of volunteers. We always try to make our helpers know how much we appreciate their assistance and how necessary they are to us. Everyone likes to know they are valuable.

Tip: Volunteers appreciate small, inexpensive, thoughtful gifts or cards. I do not think expensive gifts are appropriate.

30 RAY'S QUALITY OF LIFE

Life is precious. Eight weeks before he died of bone cancer, Jimmy Valvano, in his famous speech, said:

"To me, there are three things we all should do every day. We should do this every day of our lives. Number one is laugh. You should laugh every day. Number two is think. You should spend some time in thought. And number three is, you should have your emotions moved to tears, could be happiness or joy. But think about it. If you laugh, you think, and you cry, that's a full day. That's a heck of a day. You do that seven days a week, you're going to have something special."

Ray can do all three of these things and more. And he can move you to tears or laughter when he makes eye contact with you, or cries, or smiles, or closes his eyes to acknowledge the simple greeting of a five-year-old child. He can frighten the largest man with his scream.

With his intellect, eyes, and ears, he experiences his children growing to maturity. To some extent, we live through our children. Their successes and failures are part of our life. Walking his daughter down the aisle, as Ray did, is important to him and to her. Seeing and celebrating baptisms and graduations, as Ray has done, are important experiences. His children talk to him face to face, explaining what is going on in their life.

Ray has daily interaction with people in our home. Several people make eye contact with Ray and talk with him at church. It is thrilling to see the eyes of someone who, for the first time, suddenly realizes they can connect with him.

We attend Homecoming yearly at Harding University. Ray's college friends reminisce about their college days. Usually someone who has not seen Ray for many years will reconnect with him. He really lights up at the telling of old stories. It is one of the highlights of his life.

God has blessed us by enabling us to help Ray experience a rich life. A life that is inspiring to friends and strangers alike, at home or on the road.

I pushed Ray in his wheelchair to walk Nicole down the aisle at her wedding in 2013.

31 OUR QUALITY OF LIFE

Joshua 24:15 But as for me and my household, we will serve the LORD."

Before Ray's accident Lawana and I had plans for our present and future. Besides the possibility of a health issue for Lawana or me, we did not anticipate dealing with any catastrophic event that could alter our life. This is what we expected to do:

1. Live Christian lives.

2. Help our children and grandchildren live Christian lives.

3. Spend time with our family – especially watching our grandchildren grow and develop.

4. Travel. We had been taking annual travel vacations for several years. We had travelled to the northwestern states and into western Canada, Niagara Falls and up to Toronto and Ottawa in Canada, autumn leaf peeking and historical sites in New England, and two weeks driving around London, Bath and other places in southern England. I had spent three weeks in Ukraine on a mission trip. We began to travel well before our retirement because

we had seen other couples unable to realize their travel goals in retirement due to health issues.

5. Retire in my 60s. Possibly, as early as 62 if we could afford it. I enjoyed working, but I have always found ways to use my engineering skills in my everyday life; so retirement would not mean giving up engineering.

Early on, it was hard for us to relate to a "normal" life. Just being out in public or at church and hearing people complain about what to us seemed like petty problems was often a cause for resentment. On the other extreme, we met a family at a Brain Injury Support Group meeting whose daughter was in a much worse condition than Ray. We often find someone with a more difficult problem. Finally, we were able to reconcile our feelings to consider that everyone's own problems would always be important to them. They do not measure their daily struggles against ours just as we do not really comprehend their struggles.

Ray's accident drastically changed our circumstances. We certainly did not expect this outcome. I am reminded that the apostle Paul said he learned to be content whatever the circumstances (Philippians 4:11). If I may make a play on words, I do not think Paul was ever content to be content. By this, I mean Paul was never passively content. In verse 12, he says he has learned the secret of being content in any and every situation. Then verse 13 he says he can do everything through him who gives him strength. He wrote Philippians while he was in prison in Rome. He was not content to rot in prison. He accepted the challenge of his circumstances to pray and to work as hard as he could writing, teaching, and encouraging.

When we look at Paul's life, we see he used everything he could in every situation. He used all of his Christian traits, all of his world skills (tent making) and Roman law (He used his advantages as a Roman citizen.) to accomplish his objective. It appears his secret of being content was to use all of his resources to accomplish his objective in spite of his circumstances. Paul did not dwell on the question of why he was in a particular circumstance. He learned how to excel with what God gave him.

Naomi in the Old Testament book of Ruth is interesting to me. She moves from Bethlehem to a foreign land to escape a famine. Her husband and two sons die leaving her with two foreign daughters-in-law. The famine ends in Bethlehem, so she decides to return home. Ruth stays with Naomi and moves to Bethlehem with her. I think it is interesting that Naomi thinks God is responsible for her misfortune. In Ruth 1:11, she is bitter the Lord's hand has gone out against her. In 1:21, she says the Lord has brought misfortune on her. I think her misfortune was not from God but was the result of natural events.

Naomi and Ruth arrive in Bethlehem at the barley harvest. They immediately begin to use their resources to help themselves. Ruth ends up marrying Boaz, a kinsman redeemer, and has a son named Obed. Even though Naomi thinks God is responsible for her misfortune, she stays faithful to God. She does what she can. God blesses her with a grandson, Obed. Obed is the grandfather of King David and in the lineage of Christ.

Joseph and Job are two more examples in the Old Testament of men who suffer extreme consequences. They both stay faithful to God and excel at making the best of their circumstances.

The Word of God and its promises uphold us. Lawana says that it comforts her to know that Ray will eventually be made whole again with a new spiritual body that is free from pain and limitations. She remembers an episode from the early Star Trek TV series in which Captain Pike, a mentor to Captain Kirk and former captain of the

Enterprise, is disfigured and disabled and must exist in a motorized box. At the end of program, Captain Pike is shown as being healthy and whole again. It is only an illusion given by the inhabitants of a forbidden planet. Ray's new body will not be an illusion, but eternal.

Philippians 3:20-21 But our citizenship is in heaven. And we eagerly await a Savior from there, the Lord Jesus Christ, who, by the power that enables him to bring everything under his control, will transform our lowly bodies so that they will be like his glorious body.

We are blessed with many resources. Countless prayers are offered for us. In the beginning, two churches provide spiritual and physical help. We continue to have daily help from volunteers. We are able to ask for and receive help from our church, our friends and Ray's friends. We attend local Brain Injury Support Group meetings for information. We utilize local college and university resources.

Ray made good friendships over the years and nourished those friendships. Ray's friends have been amazing. They are a constant encouragement to Ray and us. They help financially when needed. They help fund college education for Ray's children. They are part of his weekly exercise volunteers.

Lawana's experience working with medical claims helps us understand insurance matters. I use my engineering to make several modifications or devices for his wheelchair, bed, splints, wheelchair van, travel, etc. I also design our house with several features that help us care for Ray.

We adjust our daily activities when necessary. I was serving as an elder in the church; but in 2007, I decided it would be better to resign. Lawana gave up teaching a Sunday morning ladies class. She still teaches an occasional class for the Tuesday Morning Ladies Bible Class. Probably our choices of travel destinations would be different if we were not taking Ray with us. Many people make changes as their lives evolve over the years, so we do not view these adjustments in a negative way.

So are we achieving our goals? Yes, we are:

1. We continue to be active in church.

2. We are doing our best to help our grandchildren in their Christian lives.

3. We are spending time with our family. We are actually helping our grandchildren with their education more than we ever expected.

4. We are taking one or two travel vacations every year. Most of these are cruises.

5. I was able financially to retire six months after I turned 62. This has been a big help in caring for Ray and helping us reach our other goals.

There are two major health benefits for Lawana and me. First, Ray adds tremendous purpose to our lives. Second, the physical demands keep us active and in good physical condition. I think these two benefits will add years to our lives.

Caring for Ray is a routine, albeit difficult, 24/7 job. It is similar to routine care for myself (brushing teeth, eating, getting dressed, bathing, etc.) but it is more physically demanding. As long as we concentrate on our goals, we always can take care of the routine tasks. It did take a lot of determination to learn how to travel and to get the equipment we needed to care for Ray while traveling.

People ask us sometimes how we manage; we tell them we just get up every day and do what has to be done. Our primary goal for Ray has always been to give him as normal a life as possible within the scope of his limitations. We trust in God and try to live our lives accordingly. We will never get an answer to the age-old question of "Why?" in this lifetime. Since we are able to care for him and achieve our goals, we feel secure and content in our life. The important thing is that we still have him to love.

Lesson Learned: We learned how to alter our approach to reach the goals we had originally planned.

APPENDIX

Helpful Hints and Useful Products

Since two of us are taking care of Ray daily, we have designed a log to check off each item when it is completed. Either of us can tell at a glance if everything has been done or not. Our log has five multi-use columns: Medicine, Food, Juice; Output, BM; Temperature, Weight; Workouts; Comments, Activities. Medicines, food and juice are listed by time of day so we just check these off when we do them. The other columns are blank so we write information in these as things occur. I have managed to get seven days on a single page spreadsheet. The font is small but I only have to print one page per week. These are three hole punched and kept in a binder.

A backpack hung on the back of the wheelchair is very handy to store various items:

1.   A urinal to empty his leg bag.
2.   A large doorstop for those times you are by yourself and need to prop open a door for the wheelchair.

3. A syringe with plunger to check for residuals before feeding him.

4. A plain syringe for use with the feeding tube. You cannot pour into the tube without a funnel of some kind.

5. Cans of food for meals when away from home.

6. An extra towel for drooling and a towel to keep his clothes clean during feeding.

7. An extra diaper. Changing him in the wheelchair presents a challenge but sometimes it is necessary.

8. A bottle of water.

9. Tools to adjust the wheelchair.

10. Picture ID for Ray, his insurance cards, medicine list, telephone list, guardianship papers and a letter from his doctor stating he is medically fit to travel.

11. Space is available for other items as needed.

We have only found one type of male external catheter that really works for Ray. It is a Holister brand. The light adhesive on it makes it work well. We always bring some with us when Ray is in the hospital because the others do not work well.

Ray's mouth is very dry because he breathes through his mouth most of the time. Biotene Moisturizing Gel works well for Ray.

Our van is equipped with an EZ-Lock system to anchor the wheelchair. This system is easier and quicker than tie downs. His wheelchair is equipped with a large bolt that extends downward and fits in a groove on the floor mechanism.

We have a scale on his overhead lift so we can track his weight accurately. With the scale, we can detect weight gain caused by fluid retention quickly.

When he overheats outdoors, cooling cloths are very helpful in bringing down his temperature. The crystals in them absorb extra water to extend the cooling time. Construction workers use them.

We use a solution of 50% vinegar and 50% water as a soaking agent in the urinary bags when they are not in use. We discard the unused liquid after three days.

Lantaseptic cream works well on minor skin irritations and red spots.

We use gauze sponges (2x2) from our dentist to absorb drainage around his Mic-Key button feeding tube. They are easy to cut and slide under the Mic-Key button. The loose strings in regular gauze are a nuisance. This feeding tube site is still trying to heal even after 15 years.

We have a long extension on the Mic-Key button feeding tube that we can extend over Ray's shoulder. This allows us to access the tube without disturbing his clothing.

A foot tent made from steel rods prevents the sheet and covers from laying on his feet, otherwise red spots develop on the knuckles of his toes. I had to make a foot tent because I could not find one tall enough to work with his mattress.

I have designed a simple splint to use on his right arm that is made of 1/8" steel wire with sheepskin straps and a washcloth for his hand to grasp. He can wear this through the night to hold his wrist straight. The washcloth absorbs moisture in his hand and is washable. We first worked with an outpatient occupational therapist to get his wrist straight with splints that are more complicated. He can wear the simple homemade splint longer so the gain in position is not lost.

We float Ray's heels on a Stimulite honeycomb head pillow. This protects heels, ankles and the bones around the ankles from pressure sores. Before we discovered this pillow, we were continually fighting pressure sores. Supracor is the manufacturer. They make several other products for pressure relief, but we have not used anything but the pillow. Their products are a little pricy.

An absorbent hand towel folded twice makes a good drool cloth.

Very stretchy clothes help in dressing Ray. Slacks need to stretch in both directions and have plenty of give because of his history of pressure sores on his behind. Somehow, the extra stretch reduces the pressure on this skin. Athletic pants are the only ones we have been able to find with enough stretch. Even in athletic pants, we have to search hard to find the extra stretchy ones.

Button up shirts are nearly impossible. For Nicole's wedding, Lawana was able to split a dress shirt up the back just enough to get it over his head and on his arms. The split does not show because of his back being against the wheelchair back. Long sleeve tees and polos work best. Using shirts and pants one size too large is also helpful for dressing and undressing.

We found a good source for specialty clothing items on the internet – Adrian's Closet. We have a lightweight fleece garment called a fling that fits right over his head. We wanted it open down the back, so Lawana split it and seamed the edges. For wintertime, we have a heavy weatherproof cape with a hood from another supplier of accessible clothing.

Rigid shoes are not an option with Ray because they cause pressure sores. We use soft fleece shoes and diabetic socks for his feet. We removed the rubber sole insert from the shoes so they fit the shape of his feet better.

Things That Did Not Work for Us

We heard good things about using water therapy for quadriplegics, so we bought Ray a special flotation vest. We found a pool at the local Salvation Army Boys and Girls Club that had a handicapped lift and recruited some men from our congregation. After using it four or five times, it was evident that we were making no progress and that Ray seemed to be anxious about being in the water.

I built a tilt board fashioned like the ones I saw at the therapy places. The idea is to give the patient the advantage of being on his feet – a feeling of general well-being. We were able to use it for a while but Ray's feet are too pronated for him to be able to bear his full weight.

We attended the Brain Injury Support Group for several years after Ray's accident. It was evident that the majority of those attending were in far better condition than Ray. Although they too were survivors of TBI or stroke, they had so many more of their faculties than Ray did. The problems they were discussing of finding work and interacting with family really did not apply to us. We gradually stopped going.

We bought an eye gaze machine for Ray to use for communication. Ray was never successful in using it the way he should have. In later years, when we attended a workshop and talked with vendors there about eye gaze technology, they determined the reason. Before the accident, Ray had had a radio keratotomy for his nearsightedness. The scar tissue on his eyes prevented Ray from calibrating the eye gaze machine.

Over the years, there have many braces, communication devices, etc. that just did not work for Ray. We are not afraid to try new ideas, but try to avoid anything that could actually be harmful to him.

NEWSPAPER ARTICLES

Loyal friends tough to find, tough to beat
By Rick Butler, Sports Editor, December 2000
Reprinted by permission from The Daily Citizen, Searcy,
Arkansas

I've never written a column that was intended for one person. I've never written one without knowing if that person would ever get to read it.

There's a time for everything.

I have a friend from college, now living in Tulsa, Oklahoma. One of the funniest guys I've ever met, he's one of those who brings a chuckle — sometimes a belly-laugh, just at the mention of his name.

I've been thinking about him a lot this week. About all the fun things we did in college, road trips we took with our group of friends, outings with our social club.

I had not seen Ray in at least 12 years until last March when he flew into Nashville — where I was living at the time — from Orlando — where he was living at the time.

He had come in to see the NCAA South Regional Tournament which was being held downtown.

He was there to see his beloved Tulsa Golden Hurricane. I was there to see the-Hogs. He stayed interested a lot longer than I did as Tulsa won two games in the regional while the Razorbacks bowed out with the first round loss to UNLV.

I picked him up at the airport and he looked exactly as he did 12 years before. Our conversation seemed to pick up where it had the last time we had seen each other in college.

On the ride to my house, he gave me his tips on picking up tickets at the best prices for the tournament. With the help of what has to be one of the- most understanding wives of this century, Ray has developed a knack for seeing whatever games he wants to see. And paying what he wants to pay.

His wife, Shannon, works with a major airline. Ray got used to flying [free] stand-by a long time ago. With friends from college in nearly every major city, a ride from the airport and a clean towel are about his only needs once he circles a game on his calendar.

Usually, it's following the Golden Hurricane, though he still claims to be somewhat of a Razorback fan — mainly because of UA coach Nolan Richardson's time in Tulsa.

Ray is one of the most loyal persons I've ever met. If he says he's going to do something, he's going to do it. If he says he's going to be somewhere, he's going to be there.

Friends like that are tough to beat.

On his trip to Nashville, he was — as expected — the perfect houseguest. He still had the great sense of humor and he was excited about going to the tournament together.

I actually believe he was as glad to be visiting us as he was about seeing the tournament. Until the Golden Hurricane took the court, anyway.

He played with my little girl, then proudly took his wallet out and introduced her to his three children, telling her in great detail who they were and the things they enjoyed doing.

I remembered wondering if I sounded that proud when I talked to people about my daughter.

I talked to Ray a couple of weeks ago about my coming to Tulsa for Saturday's Arkansas-Oklahoma State game. I wouldn't be able to work things out to get there, but we made plans to try to meet in Fayetteville later in the year for a Hogs' game.

Last Friday, the car Ray was driving was struck from behind while he was sitting still. The impact knocked his car into an intersection, where it was struck two or three more times.

Ray is now in a coma.

He has some involuntary movement in his arms and legs, but brainstem injuries are probably more frightening than they sound.

The understanding wife and three precious children are not sure what happens now. Doctors have said he could be in a coma for a month, maybe more.

I'm praying he gets to have Christmas with his family — even if it's late. I'm hoping he gets to show those pictures of his children to more people.

I would like to see another basketball game with him. And I hope he gets to read this.

Soon.

Ray Duwe is alive

By Jason Collington, World Staff Writer, April 22, 2002
Reprinted by permission from the Tulsa World

For as long as he can, his father will make sure his son's life is one worth living

Bill Duwe knows his son Ray is in there -- in that body of stiff legs, tight fists and drawn-in arms.

That's why Bill Duwe is working on an escape.

Maybe the bars are too close together and too strong for 36-year-old Ray Duwe to completely break out.

Maybe the better bet is for him to sneak little signs of life through the cage that slammed shut after a car accident almost two years ago.

Whatever happens, Bill will wake up each day with one mission in mind. The 61-year-old is going to help his son chip away at those bars that doctors say aren't likely to budge much.

Bill has never been the type to dwell on anything negative too long. Complications from his son's brain-stem injury are no exception.

Bill's wife Lawana admits there's one big difference between her and her husband when it comes to their son's immobile condition.

She's the pessimist.

Bill is the optimist.

Back home to stay

When it's time for bed, Ray is pushed in his wheelchair past pictures of his three children hanging in the hallway.

Sometimes Ray looks at the pictures of his children, Travis, 9; Nicole, 8; and Raychel, 5, as he passes by.

Sometimes he can't. As he's ushered down the hallway by his father, his mother follows close behind.

Tonight, she's in charge of the crane. It looks strong enough to pull the motor out of a car.

Lawana cranks, lifting her 190-pound son from his wheelchair before lowering him into a bed fit for a hospital.

Ray is back in his old bedroom in his small Broken Arrow neighborhood, the one he grew up in as a kid.

A lot is different now. He's no longer in the home that was built for this wife and family just months before the accident. He's no longer at his job.

Everything changed as quickly as Ray used to swing a softball bat. He was just blocks away from his room, down the street and over a bit. He was on his way to his parents' house to pick up Travis for his first basketball practice.

While he was waiting for the car in front on him to turn left, Ray's Toyota Camry was hit from behind, putting a stop to Ray's ability to do almost anything for himself. Except breathe.

The one everyone leans on

"We're confident he's aware. He's what they call locked-in," Bill said. "He's in there, but he's not able to get out."

"But I think it's just a matter of time."

When Ray could move his left leg a little, Bill rigged together a long switch connected to the TV remote, giving Ray the chance to channel surf. Ray clicked away.

He even waited for some commercials to end to see what was on. He eventually stopped on the St. Louis Cardinal game and watched it all. He always loved the Cards.

But he doesn't move that leg anymore.

"You can get caught up in the tragedy and keep looking back, but I don't," Bill said. "I know that the only change my son will make is improvement."

That's what drives Bill every day, his wife believes. He's always looking forward, always thinking how he can improve the quality of his son's life.

"Bill's always been the one everyone's leaned on," Lawana said. "There have been times my belief in God, Jesus and the Bible don't have the ability to comfort me. Only he can."

Those who have known Bill aren't at all surprised that he never stops thinking up ways for his son to interact with his three kids.

"I have not seen bitterness," explained Bill Keele, the pulpit minister at Broken Arrow Church of Christ, where Bill Duwe is an elder. "I've seen frustration but not bitterness.

"I think his love for Ray takes the bitterness away."

As a kid, Tim Murdock who gives Ray physical therapy each day said father and son are a lot alike.

They both like to win.

Although the two can't reconnect those accident-torn blood vessels and nerves near Ray's brain, they're working together to keep his muscles strong, keeping his body in shape until the day Ray takes over control, although studies show that most people who are locked-in never do.

`He holds me up'

Because of the accident, Travis never made it to that first basketball practice.

But Travis and the other kids see Ray every other weekend and during church services. They stay the rest of the time with their mother, Shannon.

Having them and old friends around do a lot for Ray, his parents said. He perks up when they see them. "You can tell in his eyes he's listening and happy," his mom said.

Since the accident, Lawana admits she's leaned on her husband a lot. Sometimes she still screams and cries and asks why. She struggles with the fact Ray will probably outlive she and her husband. It's hard for her to see young families together.

"But he holds me up," she said of Bill. "He stays positive when I can't see how."

A smile to be thankful for
By Ashley Parrish, World Staff Writer, November 28, 2002
Reprinted by permission from the Tulsa World

Two years after a paralyzing car accident, a man's smile gives a lift to friends and family.

It's been a tough year for Nebraska football. But these years don't come around often, so a Sooner fan like Ray Duwe has to make the most of them.

Just the word "Cornhusker" makes him smirk.

"Come on, Ray, they're not even playing a state team," Daniel Wink says, referring to his beloved Nebraska's weekend game. "You're not turning Buffalo on me, are you?"

Duwe smiles on. Colorado is almost as hated as Nebraska. But not quite enough to make Duwe want to root against them when Nebraska is the foe.

The conversation goes on for an hour, as Wink lifts Duwe onto a large padded table and starts stretching his legs out in front of him.

There aren't any more smiles, because this is work. But there is an easy companionship between the two men who once worked together.

This is why Wink is thankful today.

His friend is smiling.

A dark Christmas: It's been two years since the accident.

Just down the road from his parents' Broken Arrow house, Duwe was in a car accident as he was going to pick up his young son.

His brain stem snapped. No bruises. No broken bones.

Just a crippling blow to the neck.

His family spent Christmas in the intensive-care unit at St. Francis Hospital.

His mother brought homemade rolls. His grandmother made a pie. The other patients' families filled in the rest and his father said the prayer.

It was a hopeful time, because no one knew what the future would bring.

By the next Thanksgiving, everyone knew.

While his parents said grace over a huge turkey, Duwe sat in his wheelchair in front of the television. His mother, Lawana, tried to give him a bit of pie later, but it slowly dribbled out of his mouth.

Christmas was more of the same.

Duwe could communicate without words. He was trapped inside a body that was in a constant state of atrophy, but he could nod or shake his head.

And he could cry.

He lost his wife. The chances that he would ever do anything for himself again were poor at best.

There were things to be thankful for last year, though.

There was his parents' church, Broken Arrow Church of Christ. And Duwe's own congregation, Crosstown Church of Christ, where he'd been a member for just a week before the accident. And his work friends from Hilti.

They were helping in so many little ways. Monetarily, of course, but mostly with time. They came to help his parents give him physical therapy. Building ramps. Fixing up a van.

But it was all so heart-wrenching. For his parents and for the volunteers who got so little feedback from their friend.

Then, just a few months ago, he smiled.

And everyone knew this Thanksgiving would be hopeful again.

ABOUT THE AUTHOR

Bill Duwe and his wife of 53 years, Lawana, are caregivers for their son, Ray. Sixteen years ago, Ray suffered a brainstem contusion in a motor vehicle accident that left him a non-verbal quadriplegic.

Bill is a retired engineer. His engineering experience in design of mechanical products has been very useful in building, modifying, and maintaining Ray's medical equipment. When Bill served in the Oklahoma National Guard, he received combat medic training at Fort Sam Houston. He has put this medical training to use in everyday care of Ray.

Bill and Lawana reside in Broken Arrow, Oklahoma. In addition to Ray, they have a daughter, six grandchildren, and one great-granddaughter. Bill was an elder at the church of Christ in Broken Arrow, Oklahoma for twenty-two years.

If you would like to contact Bill, he has a Facebook account.

Made in the USA
Columbia, SC
09 May 2020

95992720R00083